SILENT
MEOW

An unwanted kitten and a man suffering from a tragedy save each other

Linda C Marchman

ISBN: 153977578X
ISBN 13: 9781539775782

ACKNOWLEDGEMENTS

Several people deserve special recognition for their help in the writing process of "Silent Meow." As in my first book, "Gone Astray," Rex Marchman, Jewell Bailey, and Jane Barr, the "Comma Queen," offered timely and crucial information to make this book the best it could be. My sincere appreciation is for their encouragement and support. Thank you!

Ron Martin designed the cover, which portrayed exactly what I had requested.

To my friends, those known and unknown, who read "Gone Astray," and urged me to write another book about cats, I offer you this second book.

I dedicate "Silent Meow" to those who have ever loved a cat and received love in return.

TABLE OF CONTENTS

Proverbs 12:10 "A righteous man cares for the needs of his animal..."

Lighthouse Point is a fictitious place but may resemble small towns located on the Potomac River or Chesapeake Bay in Maryland. Life revolved around the water, with fishing, crabbing, oystering, boating and relaxing as its main pastimes or sources of people's livelihoods. Church activities figured prominently in many people's social lives as the primary source of community contact, besides that of their families. In the 1600s European Catholic settlers had landed in the area. Other religious groups began forming congregations. Nearby St. Mary's City is thought to be the birthplace of religious freedom in North America.

Captain John Smith explored the region and wrote in his journal that the "oysters lay as thick as stones" and his crew was amazed at the large numbers of fish and other edible sea creatures available. That bounty is no longer in evidence today. Overharvesting and overfishing have depleted the variety of seafood available, and those species that do survive no longer occur in the numbers that so amazed Smith's crew.

Leonardtown is a real town of several thousand residents, with a sleepy demeanor, but with a growing population.

All of the events in "Silent Meow", all of the characters, and their names are products of the author's imagination. One exception is "Aunt Evonne," who is a real person. The family names Gass, Talbot and Calvert are historically common in the area depicted.

Tropical Storm Brenda developed in the Gulf of Mexico on July 2, 1960 and continued its journey across Florida. It then became an official tropical storm and headed up the east coast of the United States, with winds of 60 mph. It tracked over the Chesapeake Bay, crossed southeastern Maryland and on up into New England. No direct casualties were reported, except for one traffic-related death.

1

THE FAMILY

In the early 1960s, in a small town in Southern Maryland, where the Potomac River meets the Chesapeake Bay, and bits of land poke into the water like wet fingers, a family was taking in the first rays of the day's sunshine. It was early summer and the heat had yet to penetrate the air to make it heavy with the humidity that sucks the spirit out of a person's psyche. A rickety dock with grey-weathered wood jutted out about 100 feet into the water. Rusty nails stuck out from where the boards joined the underpinnings, making it an obstacle course for anyone walking barefoot. A few boards had disintegrated over the years, leaving gaps and adding to the hazard.

The family sunning itself at the dock's end was a furry one. A large black and white tuxedo cat, a female, stretched her long and languid form and reached for a scruffy black kitten, just beyond her grasp. The kitten jumped backward, almost tumbling into the water, but hung on enough to right himself. He then crouched, jiggling his backside, and pounced on the female's tail. The tuxedo swiped without extending her claws at the mischievous kitten and they ended up in a playful ball of fur. A smaller gray and white kitten watched the show from several feet away.

All of a sudden, the larger cat's attention focused on a metal cage, which was suspended a few feet below the waterline. It held a crab with bright blue claws and an olive-colored shell that grappled with a shredded chicken neck. Its pointy claws grasped the neck and tried to maneuver it into a more favorable position. Fascinated with the crab, the three cats hung over the side of the dock, flicking their tails in anticipation. The crustacean scrabbled and scraped, trying to find the exit, to no avail, and then settled down with the chicken neck to eat its breakfast.

The cats were hungry and wanted a bit of chicken, too. They knew instinctively that they should not jump in the water, but the spectacle of the crab was very enticing. The tuxedo extended her arm so her paw lightly touched the water. The crab paid no attention to her. But the black kitten, whiskers twitching and bright eyes round with awareness, was determined not to let this opportunity pass him by. His hair stood on end and he resembled a miniature spooky Halloween furball. He launched himself into the water, intent on the crab's cage. Sinking quickly into the water's depths, he panicked, unable to breathe. Squirming underwater, he slowly rose to the surface, fur plastered to his skinny body. Looking like the proverbial drowned rat, he sputtered and cried, a pitiful meeoow to which his mother responded helplessly.

The kitten pawed at the air in vain before sinking down again uttering a pathetic watery squeak. The mother cat became frantic, running back and forth on the dock, with a wild look in her eyes. Her kitten surfaced once more, noticeably weaker. Fear for her baby became greater than her fear of the water, and the mother launched herself off the dock. She was startled and confused at the strange sensation of the liquid surrounding her body. Near panic as her head submerged, instinct kicked in and she was able to paddle toward the wayward kitten. Grabbing him around the scruff of his neck with her mouth, she then proceeded to begin her awkward swim toward the shore. The youngster hung limply underneath his mother's chest, head above water, as she stroked her way slowly toward safety. Navigating some grass, she finally found a foothold in the mud and clambering up a short incline, laid the black one on the ground. Panting and tired, she knew her job wasn't over. She began licking her kitten all over, trying to stimulate him and bring some life back to him. The ground was littered with whole and broken oyster shells, which hurt the cat's paws. But she continued to lick the salt water off him until he opened an eye and stared at her.

Meanwhile on the dock, the other kitten walked silently down towards her sibling and mother. She had been scared being left alone when her mother plunged into the water and she was now visibly upset but didn't say a word. She stood mute as she watched the tuxedo revive her brother. She was a timid and ordinary kitten in terms of coloring. Her gray and white stripes were patterned typically like those of a tabby. This bit of fluff never meowed or verbally expressed any emotion, but her eyes always gave her emotions away. Animated and large for her tiny face, they could convey feelings that she was unable to show otherwise. Her eyes were a bluish green, dramatized by dark eyeliner, but she was active when the situation required it, watchful and alert in observing her surroundings.

Not too far away and half buried in the sand and muck was an old overturned boat. Its upside down bow was protruding higher than the rest. A tattered and decaying rope was tied to a corroded ring on the front and was buried in the sandy dirt. Green paint was peeling, but the name, "Taffy" was still somewhat legible on one side. The cats weren't interested in the boat, but sometimes they hid under it when necessary.

The smell of the bay lingered in the air; it was not unpleasant, but had a distinctive fishy odor. A few fish bones were strewn on the ground, bleached white by the sun. On one of the pilings, a seagull perched, seemingly unafraid of the cats below him. He ruffled his feathers and took wing, heading out to find something to eat.

As the black kitten was drying and regaining his life essence, the female tuxedo began to wash herself to rid her fur of the salty smell and taste. The sun rose higher and the day warmed. It promised to be a perfect summer day for the cats now that the emergency was over and they quickly settled into the contentment of the moment. The only lingering effect was a fortunate one, in that the kitten was now aware that jumping off the dock was not a good idea, no matter how tempting a prize was in the crab trap.

At about the same time that the cat family was recovering from their morning's adventure, a middle aged man started heading toward the dock from his house, just up the lane. Carrying his tackle box and his fishing pole, he was a familiar sight in the neighborhood on sunny mornings. Dressed in faded jeans, a floppy hat, and a worn t-shirt purchased in Ocean City, Maryland years before, he was headed to one of his favorite places. If the fish weren't biting, he was usually rewarded with a few blue crabs that he caught in his trap. Other folks who lived in the hamlet knew that the trap was his and didn't raid it to remove his bounty.

As he strolled along, he wore a smile and hummed a hymn from Sunday's church service. He thought the sermon had been a particularly good one, taken from the book of Job. The Bible's Job was a favorite of his. Chapter 14, verses 7-9 read, "At least there is hope for a tree: If it is cut down, it will sprout again, and its new shoots will not fail. Its roots may grow old in the ground and its stump die in the soil, yet at the scent of water it will bud and put forth shoots like a plant." The man liked to think of himself as the tree, cut down, but not defeated. For so long he actually had felt defeated but now he was regaining his mental health. He wanted to put forth more shoots in the time he had left on earth. He had cultivated patience and faith over the years and it had carried him through the bad times.

The boy was playing on the grass in a yard with a picket fence. Sporting a startling red crewcut and a striped shirt, he had a model car in hand and was pretending to race it through the dirt. As the man walked by, the boy looked up and said, "Good morning, Reverend Maye."

"And a fine morning it is, Teddy," came the reply. "Glad to see you back in church."

"Yeah, my mom made me go."

The Reverend chuckled and said, "Do you want to do a little fishing this morning?"

Teddy looked hopeful but then he remembered something. "No, I can't. My mom wants me to go with her to Leonardtown to do some shopping. But I'd rather go with you."

"Well, maybe another time. Have fun shopping."

The boy wrinkled his nose and then waved goodbye.

The sandy road ended abruptly before it turned into a shell pathway leading to the dock. On one corner was a neighborhood grocery store/Post Office that served the tiny community. The hand-painted sign on the store's front read, "Lighthouse Point Grocery." Two wooden benches flanked the door. Above one of the benches, a metal Hires Root Beer sign complete with thermometer had been tacked to the weathered wall. It served as a gathering place for old men to swap stories of past fishing triumphs and tragedies, and for children to sit, with strict orders to stay put, while sipping their Orange Crushes. A rusting coffee can with sand in the bottom contained discarded cigarette butts. Inside, canned goods, bait, tackle, cereal, milk and sundries lined the shelves. In the back corner of the store stood a slot machine, a happy distraction in a town with little in the way of entertainment. The slot machine did a brisk business, making short work of a roll of nickels. Occasional wins of ten or twenty dollars encouraged players to persist, although the usual payouts did not reward the gambler as handsomely as was hoped for. Even children played the slot machine, but usually without the permission of their parents. The children were more interested in the old ice cream freezer that offered Good Humors, Dreamsicles and frozen pops that sold well on those steamy summer days.

Leaving his tackle box and pole leaning against the building, Reverend Andrew Maye strode up the few steps and opened the creaky screen door of the store. He didn't see Rosie anywhere as he walked back to the cooler and took out a cold soft drink. Rosie didn't appear so he just left some change on the counter and walked out, retrieving his fishing gear. Rosie was the owner of the store and she lived in the rooms above it. She had lived there with her husband until his death in an accident a decade earlier, but now lived alone, except for her granddaughter, Veronica, who came to visit on weekends and during summer vacation.

As early as it was, there were not many people out and about. The Reverend liked this time of day when everything seemed new and fresh. He breathed in some salty air and thought about how much he liked living in this little dot on the map. Years ago, when he resided in the suburbs of Washington, DC, he never thought one day he would be a minister in a small church close to the Chesapeake Bay. The traffic, the crowds, the houses with tiny yards were now just a memory and it seemed like a lifetime ago that he and Taffeta decided to chuck it all and move. And now, Taffeta was just a memory. But as long as he remembered her, she was still alive, if not in person, but in spirit. He tried to think of the good things and suppress the bad thoughts that always brought on those painful headaches and deep depression.

Across the road, set back from the road was a Methodist church. A dirt driveway led up to a grassy parking area. On one side was a flower bed with many species of blooming roses. One could see that the church grounds were well-maintained, with closely-cropped grass edging the walkway. The wooden sign read, "Lighthouse Point Methodist Church, Established 1892." This was Andrew Maye's church.

Turning down the oyster shell pathway, he passed a weeping willow tree with delicate leaves, brushing the sand. The tree, which had been planted as part of the church's 50th anniversary celebration, provided graceful curves to complement the church's straight symmetry. On the other side was a pretty mimosa tree, festooned with fragrant pink flowers, glowing in the morning sun. Ah, nature's perfume! A few butterflies flitted about the tree, feeding on the flowers' nectar. At one time there had been a house situated close to the water, with its inhabitants enjoying the sight of both trees. In fact, he could see the outline of a foundation where the house had stood. He remembered what had happened, why the house was gone, and quickly pushed the memory away. Continuing down toward the water, he saw some movement near the dock. He recognized the three cats who seemed to make their home nearby. The little black one was lying on the ground, with the larger black and white one hovering over him. The gray and white kitten was grooming herself on the dock. Andrew liked cats and enjoyed seeing them play on the dock when he was fishing. He usually brought them a snack and today he had some leftover chicken from last night's dinner in his metal box. As he approached, the cats looked up and came running over to greet him. They rubbed his ankles and blocked his way until he reached down to stroke each one. He knew these weren't feral cats; they were just strays who didn't belong to anyone.

"Well, good morning to you!" Two cats meowed back at him. The white and gray one just turned her face to the sun as if to greet it.

"Are we hungry this morning?" he asked. He already knew the answer. "Let's see what I have for you today."

He set his box on the ground, opened it and removed the chicken he had wrapped up in a napkin. The cats danced as they sniffed the delicious aroma. Chicken was one of their favorites. He spread the napkin on the ground and all three cats grabbed the pieces, seemingly without even chewing the meat. He had brought enough so they would at least have a good meal for the day. Having done his duty by the cats, he walked to the end of the dock and began to set up his equipment. He hardly glanced at the old boat partly covered by the sand.

He removed a paper container from his box that held a few dozen live crickets. Their movement attracted the attention of the cats who scurried down the dock to investigate. The black one instantly began to paw at the carton, moving it toward the edge of the dock. Andrew quickly picked it up and replaced it in his tackle box.

"Oh no you don't. How will I catch any fish if we feed all the bait to them right away?" he asked the kitten. There was no answer. "Ok, I'll give you one to play with." He reached in the container and grabbed a cricket by the legs and threw it down. The cats immediately ran towards it and the cricket promptly jumped into the water. With his focus entirely on the cricket, the black kitten almost ran off the edge of the dock until Andrew grabbed him and pulled him back.

"Boy are you ever a live wire! Hasn't anyone told you that cats don't like to swim? I don't want you to drown this morning and I sure don't want to have to jump in to save you. If you'll go find something else to do while I catch some fish, there might be a snack for you in the deal."

Trying to ignore the cats, the reverend began to bait his hook and then cast the line in the water. The black one perked up at the splash but didn't try to jump in. Instead he focused on the crab pot, now that it held three crabs. Leaning over the dock's side, he watched them scrabble around, trying to escape. Thinking back on his last watery misadventure, he decided to stay dry and joined his sister and mother who were relaxing on the dock, paws tucked under their chests, enjoying the warmth of the sun.

This day turned out to be a bit different from his usual fishing expeditions. After several hours of fishing, he had caught a nice striped bass that would make a tasty dinner. Making a mental note to use that special lure again that he had found in his tackle box, he headed home to work on Sunday's sermon. After having walked halfway home, he was surprised to notice the gray and white kitten following him. Andrew was anxious that she wouldn't be able to find her way back to her family, but since he lived just down the lane he thought he would be able to carry her back if necessary. The other two stayed in their positions on the dock, napping.

Arriving at his cottage, he found his notepad and a pencil and sat down at a small table on the back porch. He lived in the cozy but comfortable parsonage that featured a view of the water from his back yard. The kitten sat close to him and sometimes played with the grasshoppers that sprang up occasionally, and then returned to his side. As he wrote, he regarded the feline and marveled at her perfect posture, as she sat like an Egyptian cat statue, and her flexibility, as she did her cat yoga. Her face was intelligent, her expression alert, and her fur felt fine and soft to his touch when he reached down to pet her. He was partial to cats but had never owned one. Taffeta had been a cat person and had a tender heart when it came to giving a stray a meal. They had discussed the possibility of adopting a cat sometime, but the opportunity never arose, especially since they both were so busy. If things had turned out differently, they would probably have found a cat to live with them instead of having children.

As he was semi-daydreaming, he heard a knock at his front door. He walked through his house to find his friend, Samuel, grinning at him from the front porch.

"Andy! I've been looking for you!" Samuel exclaimed. "I didn't see you on the dock and you weren't at the church." Samuel wore paint-stained khakis and a shirt that had seen better days, appropriate attire for the handyman tasks he had been doing at the church. His graying hair was concealed under a cap and his hands were calloused. Older than Andrew, and with a pleasing expression on his face, he was a much loved fixture in the community of Lighthouse Point. Samuel was a naturally active man, having spent his younger life working on a fishing boat, and had no interest in the kind of retirement where you sit in your house and watch television. Taking care of the church building and grounds provided just enough challenge and activity to keep him busy, while still allowing time to fish and to relax with friends. This life suited him, and his contentment was evident in his calm and agreeable manner.

"Well, I caught my dinner this morning and now I'm in back working," Andrew told him.

"I just wanted to let you know that there's a leaking faucet in the women's restroom and I can't seem to fix it. Do you want me to call Clyde?" Clyde was the neighborhood plumber.

"You might as well. Have him look at the sink in the back room too." Andrew paused and then said, "Do you want to come in for a glass of tea?"

"Yeah, that sounds good. I promised Claudia I would fix our gutter this morning, but I have a few minutes."

Andrew and Samuel made their way back to the neat kitchen where Andrew poured Samuel a cold glass of sweet tea. They took their glasses out on the back porch where the kitten was still waiting. She looked up expectantly.

"And who is this little ball of fur?" Samuel asked.

"She is one of the strays that hangs around the dock, hoping for a handout. Her mother is that kind of black and white cat that looks like someone dressed in a tuxedo, with a white shirt front under a black out-fit, and her brother is a frisky black kitten. I thought he was going to fall in the water this morning, trying to catch one of my crickets. This little one is much more civilized."

"Are you going to take her in?"

"Well, no, I hadn't planned to. She just followed me home this morning. I'm not sure that I want a cat, but she certainly does behave herself."

The kitten made herself comfortable close to the men's feet as they discussed other church matters. Samuel Gass had grown up in Lighthouse Point and had been a member of the Methodist church ever since he was a boy. His family was still living in the area and most of them also attended Andrew's church. It was that long-term involvement which had led Samuel to become the unofficial caretaker after he retired. When he mowed the church's cemetery yard, he walked among the graves of his ancestors. When he made a repair in the sanctuary, he saw the pews where earlier generations of the Gass family had prayed.

"I'd better be on my way. Claudia will be back from shopping in Leonardtown soon, so I'd better get started on that gutter."

Samuel pushed his chair back and as he did, one chair leg unfortunately landed on the kitten's tail. The men watched as she opened her mouth to squeal but no sound was forthcoming. She jumped up, swishing her wounded tail and scurried off without making any noise. Andrew watched her closely.

"She didn't say anything at all," he mused. "I've never heard her meow. I wonder if she can."

"I'm so sorry! I hope I didn't hurt her." Samuel sheepishly responded.

"I think she'll be ok. I'll check on her later. Thanks for stopping by."

"Ok. I'll come by in the morning to see about pruning the rose bushes."

Meanwhile, the little tabby ran all the way back to the dock and wrapped herself around her mama. The kitten smelled different, from having been inside Andrew's house, so her mother cleaned her carefully before they both settled down to nap together.

2

GEORGETOWN

They had met in Washington, DC. The war had helped to produce jobs in the DC area and the man and the woman took advantage of this bonus. She was working as a bookkeeper in a clothing store in Georgetown and he had a civilian office job. It was a pleasant early summer day and she had decided to eat her lunch outdoors near the C&O Canal. She was sitting on a bench, watching the ducks swim past. He was walking toward her, admiring her blonde hair as it caught the sun's rays and reflected a golden glow, like a sparkling waterfall. A tall man with dark wavy hair, he could make young women turn their heads as he passed by. His dark eyes sported long lashes, a bit unusual for a man. Andrew was a straightforward, considerate young man, and the fact that he never realized how handsome he was only added to his appeal. In high school he had been shy, and never had the time or money for much dating, but he was determined to change that now that he was out on his own. And here was his opportunity, in the form of a golden-haired vision, to start his new way of life. He slowed down a few steps before he reached her and then stopped at her bench. The air was faintly scented, as if from cherry blossom trees, but there were none around. Andrew hadn't ever thought about believing in fate, but it seemed as if everything was conspiring to attract him to this lovely woman. She looked up and smiled at him as he asked, "Do you mind if I sit here?" She gestured by patting the bench beside her and continued to eat delicately, taking small bites and chewing slowly. He sat but was at a loss for words.

"Nice day, isn't it?" he finally asked her, since he couldn't think of anything else to say.

She smiled again and nodded as she continued to eat her lunch. He glanced at her from the corner of his eye and admired what he saw. She was slim, well-dressed and moved gracefully. She was delicate in the way she ate, using her napkin to dab at her mouth. A strand of blonde hair blew lazily in the breeze. He tried to think of something else to say.

He pointed at the ducks and inquired, "Do you come here often?" Again, he was fumbling to say something clever, or at least produce an ice-breaker that wasn't such a cliché.

She again nodded her affirmation.

He began to wonder why she hadn't said anything when he asked questions. Her lack of oral response was puzzling.

"I'm Andrew. What's your name?" he asked.

She put down the uneaten part of her sandwich and looked right in his eyes. She drew a line across her mouth with her finger and shook her head. So, she didn't or couldn't speak. He stared at her for a second and then, self-consciously, cocked his head to one side.

"Ok then, I can talk for both of us. Some people say I talk too much anyway." He thought a minute and then asked, "Do you have some paper and a pencil?"

She nodded and reached in her purse and took out a small notebook and pencil. She jotted the words, *My name is Taffeta.*

"Taffeta! What an unusual name! Do people call you 'Taffy' as a nickname?"

She nodded and smiled at him. He liked her smile and her straight white teeth.

She wrote, *I have to go back to work.*

"Well, I need to go back also. Where do you work?"

She wrote down the name of the store and stood up to leave.

"Maybe I'll see you again sometime."

She nodded and turned and walked away. He watched her flowery dress swing as she walked away. He was already planning ways to see her again.

3

MISCHIEF

The gray and white kitten had been taking it easy, staying close to her mother. Her tail still hurt from where the chair leg had landed on it, but it wasn't broken or swollen. She thought back to how she had followed the man to his house that morning. She knew he liked cats since he always brought them something to eat. She wanted to spend some more time with him and that's why she followed him home. After all the morning's excitement, she decided that taking a nap would help to calm her and that's what she did, curled up on the dock.

Meanwhile, her brother was trying his best to find mischief. A honeybee buzzed around the clover, making an appealing moving target for the curious kitten. He jumped up and pounced on the bee, which promptly stung him on his face. The little feline yelped and jumped backward, rubbing his face with his paw. He raced around as the venom penetrated his skin. Mama cat came running over to see what was wrong. The black one frantically pawed at his wound, while his mother licked his face, trying to soothe the hurt. His face started to swell and he began to look a bit deformed. His tongue lolled out and a bit of foam formed around his mouth. He moaned as his mama tried to comfort him. He lay down in the grass waiting for the pain to go away, still pawing at his face.

Other than the trouble her brother got into, life on the dock was pleasant for the kitten and her family. On bright days, the cats spent most of their time whiling away the hours sunning. If it was hot, they took shelter underneath a shrub or under the porch of the store. On rainy days, they found a place under the old boat. The woman from the store and this morning's fisherman weren't the only people who occasionally brought them food, and there were always mice to catch. It was a simple life, one that she expected to go on forever.

Later on, after the sun had peaked and was following its arc toward the horizon, the cats became active. It had been a good day. Neither kitten remembered the trouble they had gotten into. Hungry again, they sauntered toward the store, where Rosie sometimes left food for them on the porch. This afternoon, a bowl of leftover fried fish awaited them. The smell was irresistible and they scarfed down the tidbits. Sitting on their haunches, they licked themselves all over so they could still smell the scent of the fish. It had been a good day for the most part, except for the trouble the little black mischief-maker had been into.

The moon began to show its face. It was full and had a bewitching effect on the cats. It illuminated the landscape like the land of the midnight sun, but with a softer haziness. The night creatures around the water could feel it also. There seemed to be more activity, more noise, and more eyes shining in the shadows than usual. Small insects' eyes that were unremarkable in the daylight shone like tiny jewels. Resembling miniature car headlights, the eyes loomed out of the darkness in shades of red, pale yellow and luminescent green. Casting an eerie glow, the moonshine was diffuse but also soothing and comforting for the cats after the brightness of the day. The cats loved this time of the night when they could hunt.

A barely perceptible squeaking roused all three of them. The peeping was coming from under the boat and they began to creep toward it. A rustling came from the nearest side and then the cats picked up the odor of the mouse. Their tails began to swish back and forth in anticipation. Crouched on the sand and crushed oyster shells, they all pricked their ears forward and their whiskers were on full alert. Then, without further ado, the black kitten scrunched down underneath the boat to capture his prize. The wary mouse saw him coming and scurried back toward the scrubby grass and disappeared on the other side of the boat. At that moment, the boat slightly tilted toward the side where the other two cats were watching and the kitten was trapped beneath the boat.

After a moment the little one realized his predicament and began crying. This upset the mother cat and she began pacing around the boat's perimeter, trying to soothe her baby who was trapped and out of reach. Minutes passed and the female tuxedo cat became increasingly frantic as she heard her kitten whimpering. She jumped on top of the boat, which made it sink a bit deeper into the sand, but the attempt to free her kitten was useless.

Hours of darkness passed and the moon cast a glow on the cat family crowded around the boat. The black kitten's desperate cries became softer until they ceased altogether. The mother cat continued to cry loudly as she raced around the boat, trying to dig her kitten out. The tide started to come in.

4

LIGHTHOUSE POINT

Andrew and Taffeta were married about a year after that first enchanting meeting at the Canal. There had been a lot of activity in the Washington DC area. New homes were being built in the suburbs of Virginia and Maryland, but the newly married couple chose to live in Georgetown in a small rented row house. Taffeta continued to work as a bookkeeper in the clothing shop and Andrew was promoted in his job. She taught him sign language and she was able to communicate well with him, although he usually spoke to her orally. She had been mute since her birth and was used to conveying her thoughts through gestures, writing and facial expressions. Andrew had asked her why she was unable to talk, but Taffeta indicated that her parents had her examined by a doctor when she was a small child, but were told that the defect was just something she was born with and couldn't be remedied.

Taffeta had taken piano lessons when she was younger. Music allowed her to express the emotions that she had not been able to voice. Playing the piano was almost like learning and using a different language, which she enjoyed. She could play the instrument with authority and her fingers moved gracefully up and down the keyboard. Classical pieces were her favorite, but she had learned some jazz music and a few tunes from the big band era.

The streetcars had ceased operating so the couple usually walked to wherever they needed to go. More people were driving automobiles but Andrew and Taffeta hadn't purchased one yet. A laundromat was down the street, a small restaurant served decent food, and a neighborhood grocery store was within walking distance. They loved living in Georgetown, where they admired the architecture, the quaint streets and the well-tended gardens. Life was satisfying for both of them.

Andrew encouraged Taffeta to take classes at Gallaudet, the college that served primarily hearing impaired students. She was reluctant at first, since she had a difficult time when she was attending classes years before in the public schools. Her lack of speech was a constant embarrassment to her and her anxiety level increased as she was unable to speak in language that hearing people could understand. But after some coaxing, she enrolled and chose a few arts-related courses. She excelled at art and was also able to practice the piano on a second hand one at the school. She blossomed at Gallaudet. She sparkled in her new marriage, living with Andrew, a man she adored, working part-time and going to college.

Sometimes on Sunday, they would attend worship services at a nearby Methodist church. Occasionally they would make the effort to go to National Cathedral. The Cathedral, built on top of a hill, was one of the most impressive buildings they had ever seen. Resembling a European cathedral, they admired its majestic Gothic architecture, the stained glass windows and its towers.

Andrew took a special interest in the workings of the church and became drawn to the Bible. He could stay engrossed in its pages for hours, trying to decipher the real meaning of Jesus's words and his parables. The minister at the local Methodist church noticed Andrew's attentiveness and formed a friendship with him. Andrew began volunteering at the church, leading a Bible study group for adults each week. He seemed to have a knack for explaining difficult passages to others, making them see the intent and application in their lives.

After a few years, Andrew's mentor told him about a unique opportunity. There was a small Methodist church in Southern Maryland that was seeking a new minister. Because of their remote location, the church members had not been able to retain a full-time minister since their elderly clergyman had retired.

Although the hamlet was less than two hours from their Georgetown home, the rural setting seemed a world away from their current lives. Andrew and Taffeta were excited about making such an adventurous move. But if they were going to move from town to the Potomac River shore, they would need a car.

They sold a few pieces of antique furniture that had belonged to Taffeta's family. In that time, many people thought the term "antique" was just another word for "old junk." But after adding some of their savings, they finally had enough money for a down payment on a used DeSoto. Andrew found a three-year old 1949 DeSoto Custom, one of the first models to have a key-operated starter. The car was an attractive light green color with sleek rounded lines. When Andrew brought it home the first day, Taffeta clapped her hands and excitedly slid into the passenger seat. They decided to call it 'Hernando,' honoring the Spanish explorer who discovered the Mississippi River. Chrysler Motor Company had named the car after the adventurer, without knowing the full story of his exploits. The car's motor was quiet and purred like an overgrown kitten. Andrew and Taffeta drove it around the narrow streets of Georgetown, like proud parents of a newborn baby in a carriage. Driving over the picturesque arched Key Bridge, they took day trips out into the Northern Virginia countryside, toured the cobblestone streets of

Alexandria, and became more familiar with the great national buildings of Washington. Andrew showed Taffeta where he used to live with his Aunt Martha, the high school he had attended and the cemetery where his parents were buried. The car allowed them more freedom to explore than they had when they walked everywhere, but it also gave them more first-hand experience of the increasing population in the Washington area. The suburbs were growing, and they found themselves in the new traffic phenomenon called 'rush hour.' The idea of moving to a smaller, slower-paced town became even more appealing.

One weekend they decided to drive out to Lighthouse Point to look over the little settlement and visit the church where Andrew would soon be working. Leaving the Washington congestion, they headed out on Route 301 south. Both were thankful that the drive to Lighthouse Point didn't require crossing the new-ly-completed Chesapeake Bay Bridge. They'd heard it was as tall as a skyscraper and the lanes very nar-row. Taffeta thought it would be scary to look over the guardrails to the water, since she didn't swim and had no need to be in the water. They passed small intersec-tions and open farmland, with tobacco fields and corn growing in others. A handmade sign on one corner advertised 'Sweet Honey' with an arrow pointing down a country road. After they drove a few more miles, Taffy pointed out another sign. This one was attached to a front porch railing, and proclaimed 'Sewing ~

Good Prices.' These little businesses nestled among the fields gave the couple a sense of simple, uncomplicated lives in a community of friends and neighbors. This idea appealed to Andrew and Taffeta.

They came to a small produce stand, with bright flats of strawberries on display. Andrew pulled over and chatted with the farmer while buying a box of the perfectly ripe fruit. The strawberry aroma filled the car, and they couldn't resist gobbling up some right there in the parking lot. Taffeta enthusiastically agreed with Andrew's assessment that they were the best he had ever tasted, and his plan to buy some whipping cream to go with them on their way home. This rural area, such a change from their Georgetown home, was becoming more and more enticing. After turning off the main highway onto a smaller state road, Andrew slowed down so they could absorb the surroundings and the scenery. As they came closer to Lighthouse Point the sky seemed to reach down to touch the horizon and meet the water. The distinctive smell of the river wafted through the car's windows and the breeze was gentle and welcoming. The couple, who had been a little nervous at the start of their journey, found themselves relaxed and happily anticipating the sight of their new home and community.

The road took them past small ranch style homes, most with flower and vegetable gardens. A few people were out mowing their lawns and waved to Taffeta and Andrew as they passed. Every so often an old white farmhouse sat off the road, reminding people of when the land had supported whole families. The fading paint and sagging front porches implied a more prosperous era, before progress made its relentless march to a new way of life.

An insignificant sign that read "Lighthouse Point, Established 1888" told them that they had arrived in the tiny waterside community. They were mildly surprised to see how small the place actually was. No other businesses besides the general store were visible. The road dead ended with an attractive white clapboard church right in front of them.

"That's it!" exclaimed Andrew. "That's my church!" He was so excited that he parked the car right on the grass and jumped out, without thinking to walk around to open the door for his favorite passenger. He stood looking at the building, captivated by its sturdy frame and bell tower. Symmetrical with clear, arched windows, it beckoned to him. He shut his eyes for a minute and thanked God for leading him to this place.

Meanwhile Taffeta, amused and touched by Andrew's excitement, had let herself out of the car and was looking around at their new community, thinking about all the changes they would be making in their lives in the first few months, by moving to this lovely but very different place. As she was standing by the car she heard a noise behind her and turned to see a man, back by the road, watching them. He was wearing jeans and an old t-shirt that had seen better days. His hair was a mixture of brown and gray and was tousled by the wind. The man seemed to be sizing them up so she smiled at him. He returned the smile.

"Hi y'all!" he greeted them.

Andrew walked up to the man and said, "Hello! I'm Andrew Maye. I'm this church's new minister."

"Yeah, I figured that. We don't get too many cars here with Washington DC license plates. I'm Samuel Gass," as the men shook hands. "I've heard you might be coming this way to check out our little town."

"We just drove down for the day. Do you think it's possible for us to have a look inside? I think I was told there was a cottage available for us also."

"Well, sure. The door is never locked so we can go on in. I'm sort of the handyman here. I do some yard work and keep an eye on the building in case there are any problems." He turned to Taffeta and smiled again.

"I don't believe we've been introduced yet," he told her.

Andrew stepped in and said, "Oh, I'm sorry. This is my wife Taffeta. She doesn't speak, but she does communicate with gestures. She also "talks" by writing her thoughts on paper."

"Well, pleased to meet you, Taffeta. Do people call you Taffy?" he asked her.

Taffeta nodded her head in response and rewarded Samuel with a big smile.

They followed Samuel into the church building. He flipped on a light switch and a few hanging lamps illuminated the interior. Wooden pews filled both sides and a dark green carpet ran the length of the center aisle. The church smelled of the wax Samuel used on the pews that morning. The windows were plain, with no stained glass to block the sunlight.

Andrew walked down the aisle to the front and the pulpit. Behind this area were a few rows of straight-backed chairs with music stands in front of them. This was where the choir sat. He liked it right away and could imagine the parishioners on Sundays sitting in the pews, listening to him preach. He looked out at the door where they had entered and closed his eyes and offered another short prayer of thanksgiving.

He told Samuel, "Taffeta has an old family Bible that she would like to donate to the church. Do you think that would be okay? It's been in her family for many years and she thought its best use would be here in my first church assignment."

"Well, I'm sure that would be fine. We can check with a few of the older congregation members, just to make sure."

A piano was set up close to the choir area and Taffeta walked over and sat down at the keyboard. She began to play <u>What a Friend We Have in Jesus</u> and the music rang out in the empty church. She knew many hymns by heart and didn't need the sheet music to play them.

"Maybe you'd like to play during some of our Sunday services, Taffeta?" Samuel asked her.

Taffeta nodded.

"Great! I'm sure Thelma would like to take some time off." Taffeta assumed that Thelma was the current church music director.

Andrew took Samuel up on his offer to show them around the church grounds, and the threesome went through a side door. A path of pine needles led to a basketball court, and beyond that, continued into the woods. The court was old but usable, with grass sticking up through it in places. There were wooden benches where the path met the court and worn nets on the hoops. "This is where some of our teens hang out. They don't necessarily have to belong to our church, but we like to give them a place where they can feel safe and away from that blasted slot machine in the store. There's not much to do here so they sort of have to make their own fun."

As the little group circled the building, Taffeta smelled the rose garden even before it came into view. She loved the old-fashioned, heavily-scented varieties that were thriving under Samuel's care, and imagined being able to cut one to put on her dresser. Beyond the roses, they could see the headstones of the small cemetery. They saw markers dating back more than fifty years, many for members of the locally prominent Gass, Calvert and Talbot families. Everything was neat and tidy, with the grass newly mown. A white picket fence surrounded the graveyard. Andrew leaned against the fence and squinted at one particular grave. There was a pair of false teeth on the headstone.

"Old Stan Teeter always said he wanted to make sure that he had teeth in his mouth when he went to heaven. Well, when he died some years ago, the undertaker forgot to put his teeth in before sealing the casket. We all knew how mad Stan would be if he found out he had no teeth so I make sure that his choppers are always here. Of course, sometimes they disappear and we have to replace them with another set. It's probably some of those kids." Samuel told them.

The new minister and his wife smiled at this.

"Do you want to walk down to the parsonage?" Samuel asked. "I haven't been there for a while and I'm sure it needs some attention. We've only had visiting ministers for the past few months and none of them have lived there."

"What happened to the full-time minister?" Andrew inquired.

"Well, he retired, or maybe he was just tired. He had a bad heart and his daughter in Baltimore insisted that he come live with her and her husband, which was probably a good idea. He had barely been able to keep up the past few years. Some Sundays he would stand up to give the sermon and just say a few words before calling for a hymn. You could tell that he had planned to say more, but he just ran out of energy. We really needed someone to breathe some fresh air into our church and that's why when we found you, it seemed like a perfect match."

5

A NEW LIFE

Andrew and Taffeta moved in two months later. They had given notice at their jobs, had good-bye dinners with their friends, and packed all their belongings into boxes. They had never accumulated many things, preferring to live simply, so moving was relatively easy. The parsonage was fully furnished, but some of the items were very worn or not to Taffeta's taste. A small truck from a local moving company brought the few pieces of furniture that they wanted to keep from their townhouse. Once they arrived in Lighthouse Point a few of the church members helped them carry the furniture and boxes into their new house. Taffeta made iced tea and coffee for them, all of whom rushed home to tell their families about the new minister and his mute but gracious wife.

Over the course of several days and a few more trips back and forth to Georgetown, they were settling in and already starting to feel that this was their home and not just a house.

The small porch on the back afforded them a view of the water. One of their favorite times of the day was after dinner. They would sit on the porch and watch some ducks waddling across the lawn or see the fish splashing as they burst out of the water to put on a show. Once Andrew remarked that as a boy he enjoyed fishing and it might be nice if they could find a small boat to use. Taffeta was in agreement. Even though she had never been fishing, the idea of eating fresh fish was very appealing.

Andrew comfortably settled into his new role as minister of Lighthouse Point Methodist Church. He found the long-time members welcoming, relieved that they had finally acquired a congenial pastor who was willing to move to such a small community. The job was fulfilling and it seemed to him that it was Providence that had led him to this laid-back town. The women of the church were constantly bringing the Mayes homemade pies, fresh-from-the-garden vegetables and other delectable items. Taffeta honed her cooking skills and began to produce meals that helped her and Andrew put on a few pounds.

She practiced the piano at church during the week when no one was around. Thelma made it clear to her that she really would like to retire so Taffeta began taking over the duties of music director, which didn't entail much work. The few choir members were already so tuned into the old familiar hymns that it was easy for Taffeta to slip into her new volunteer job. Not being able to speak didn't seem to bother anyone and the choir came to appreciate her skills on the piano. Life was satisfying for the newcomers.

Fall weather would soon be making its appearance in Southern Maryland as the leaves on the poplar trees lost their green summer coats and turned a glowing shade of gold. The intense heat diminished and the neighbors began to spend more time outdoors, drinking in the brisk morning freshness and tidying up their gardens. Some people planted cool weather crops like turnips and lettuce. The rhythm of nature quickened a bit as if it wanted to wring every last drop of summer and savor it, even as the days grew shorter. Labor Day passed and the young people who hung around the church yard in the evenings stayed close to their homes, concentrating on homework that was assigned in fresh, new textbooks. A parade of Monarch butterflies flew lazily by, nectaring on the remaining wildflowers as they made their way southward to Mexico, where they would spend the winter.

One of Lighthouse Point's church members sold the Mayes a used fishing boat. It wasn't a large craft but it suited the couple just fine. Painted an attractive shade of green, it mimicked the corn fields so abundant in this part of Maryland. Andrew decided to give it a name and wanted to surprise Taffeta. He bought some black paint and carefully painted the letters on the side of his new acquisition.

That Saturday, he asked Taffeta if she wanted to go fishing. Since they had only taken the boat out a few times and hadn't used it to fish, she eagerly agreed. She packed some sandwiches for lunch and Andrew collected his assortment of fishing tackle and two rods. The boat was perched on the shallow bank of their property, close to the water. The freshly-painted name on the boat's side wasn't visible from the path they took. After loading the gear into the boat, Andrew told Taffeta he had a surprise for her and walked her around to the other side of the boat, where the letters clearly spelled **TAFFY**. She stopped in her tracks and just stared at it and then finally smiled and hugged her husband. She squeezed him again indicating she loved it and beamed her appreciation.

Maneuvering the boat into the shallow water was easy for Andrew as Taffeta sat on the bench in the back. They puttered slowly out into the calm and sunny day. Staying close to the bank, Andrew showed Taffeta how to cast the line near the shore, flicking her wrist to put the bait where she wanted it. After some practice, she caught on and as they drifted along, she hooked a small fish. She watched as her bobber was pulled down beneath the water line.

"Pull it up!" he instructed. "You want to hook him so he doesn't get away."

Taffeta jerked her pole up and could feel the fish thrashing, trying to free itself. As she reeled it in, the fish emerged, flopping around until it was brought into the boat, heaving as it flipped over onto Taffeta's foot. She shrugged her shoulders.

"Well, you'll have to get it off the hook. Let me show you how to grab him so you don't get finned. It's a little small so you'll have to throw it back."

The fish's scales glistened in the sunlight like small bejeweled treasures as it lay on the bottom of the boat. Somewhat disappointed, Taffeta watched as Andrew grasped the fish and showed her how to remove the hook from its mouth.

"Ok take it and gently put it back in the water."

A bit reluctantly she released her first fish.

"To be fair, you have to give it a chance to grow up. If we caught all the babies, there wouldn't be any lunkers to catch. And then we wouldn't have any fried fish for dinner."

"I wonder if we'll have any fish for dinner tonight?" she pantomimed.

"Patience is the key to successful fishing. If Job had been a fisherman, he probably would have been a good one."

Taffeta sighed.

6

HIGH TIDE

The relentless water lapped at the pilings of the dock. As the water line rose almost imperceptibly, the line of dampness moved inland across the sand. The crab pot pulled at its tether and the lone occupant was unaware of the potential impending disaster. Safe within the confines of the metal trap, the crab feasted on the remains of a chicken neck.

The black kitten was uncomfortable in the darkness and tried to dig his way out, but the shells were sharp on his paws and it was almost impossible to make any headway. He heard his mother running up and down on the underside of the boat above him, which was only making his plight worse as the boat sank even deeper into the muck.

A few more hours elapsed and the cat family was wide awake on this night of the full moon. Two watched as the water came ever closer to the overturned boat.

The wind picked up a bit and the water began to slosh toward the shore with more force. The black kitten tried once again to dig his way out from under the boat but was unsuccessful. The spongy ground became more damp as the hours passed. The trapped feline edged closer to the back of the boat, trying to stay dry. His paws were uncomfortably wet, but licking them resulted in sand on his tongue. If he had understood about the inexorable movement of the tide, he would have been even more anxious to escape. As it was, he couldn't see the water coming closer, but he was uneasy about being trapped.

The moon began to set in the west and a few streaks of daylight appeared. By now the water had risen so much that the kitten under the boat was thoroughly wet, with the water covering his legs and gradually getting higher and higher, soon to completely engulf the boat and the kitten confined in the watery tomb. He was panicking and using what was left of his scrawny voice, calling out in helpless meows. The mama cat was exhausted from her futile attempts to reach her baby, but his desperate cries revived her. She clawed at the boat and began to yowl, a heartrending screech that punctured the night.

A figure appeared on the oyster-shell path, heading toward the dock. Slowly, it made its way toward the water and the cats. Shining a flashlight ahead of it, the circle of light illuminated the shells, then the dock, then the cats, and finally the partially-submerged fishing boat.

Taking in the scene, Rosie immediately realized that there must be a kitten in trouble and her hunch was confirmed when she heard a faint noise coming from inside the boat. She began to run toward the dock.

"Oh no! Your kitten is under the boat! How will I lift it?" she demanded of the cats. The tuxedo meowed pitifully in response and ran around in frenzied circles. Wading in the water in her sneakers, she tried to pry the boat up but it was too heavy for her.

She looked for anything she could use as a crowbar, but there were no large sticks in sight. She ran back to her store as fast as she could and disappeared from sight, leaving the tuxedo cat even more frantic. She quickly reemerged, carrying a shovel. She tried digging into the sand, but water filled it and continued rising. This didn't help because the water just seeped into the void that was created. Rosie then used the shovel as a lever and upended one side so that she could see the sodden kitten's eyes staring out at her. Finally, she was able to set the boat upright and she reached in and grabbed the little black one. Almost drowned, the kitten shivered in her arms. Rosie gently squeezed water out of his fur as she cradled him. The mother cat and the other kitten watched from the dock.

Exhausted, Rosie placed the kitten beside his mother and collapsed against a piling. She watched the three furry ones as they interacted with each other.

"What would you have done if I hadn't gotten up and started making coffee? What if I hadn't heard you?" She rested, watching as the mother cat began thoroughly cleaning her kitten. The usually rambunctious furball was bedraggled and remarkably subdued. It was as if he realized that he came close to drowning. Maybe he did have a sense of how much trouble he had been in.

Rosie picked up her shovel and trudged back to the store, tired but grateful that she had been able to save a life.

7

VERONICA

Rosie had a granddaughter Veronica, nine years old, who lived only ten miles away. She visited on occasional weekends throughout the year, but her favorite thing was spending weeks at a time with her grandmother during summer vacation. By July, her normally light brown hair turned golden from the sun each summer and she wore it long, cascading over tanned shoulders. She loved the closeness of the water, the dock, and the freedom she had when she stayed with Rosie. She had a few friends in Lighthouse Point, but she was also happy to spend time alone, entertaining herself with her Barbie doll and outdoor pursuits. This summer proved to offer a special treat as she had become familiar with the kittens and their mother who hung out on the dock. She would play with them, dragging a string across the grass or providing empty boxes for them to explore.

Veronica was as curious as a cat and liked to investigate the natural world close to the grocery store. The sidewalk to the grocery's front porch, the oyster shell path to the dock, and the pine needle walkway to the church yard all radiated out from the dead end paved road, offering tempting choices for exploration. She was usually up early every morning and outside after breakfast, checking out the night's catch in the crab trap, the shoreline to see what had washed up, and whatever else caught her eye. Rosie was not worried about her because Lighthouse Point was such a safe place, where most people knew everyone else and the level of trust was high among the neighbors. There weren't many children living nearby, but they compensated by playing together without much regard for age differences. Teddy, a bit younger than Veronica, was her best friend. They spent leisurely summer days wandering the area, picking the wild raspberries, playing tag and basketball behind the church. This morning, both children were standing on the dock, watching a fishing boat carefully make its way through the reeds as it motored out, heading toward the Chesapeake.

"Reverend Andrew asked me if I'd like to go fishing with him the other day, but I had to go shopping with my mom," Teddy said.

"Maybe we can find some fishing gear and fish off the dock," Veronica told him. "Let's go in the back of the store to see if there's a pole."

The children found what they needed and took their gear to the end of the dock. They dug a few worms and baited the hook, waiting for a bite. After about two hours, they still didn't even have a nibble, so they gave up.

Veronica asked, "How about if we meet after dinner tonight and spy on the big kids at the church?"

"Yeah, that sounds like a good idea!" Teddy told her.

The summer's light was fading as two boys bounced a basketball and tried to sink it in a handmade goal attached to a tree trunk. A girl with curly brown hair and a lanky sunburned boy with freckles sat together on a bench, holding hands and whispering to each other. A dim light glowed from a back window of the church, illuminating a patch of concrete. More young teenagers arrived, some carrying lightweight plastic-webbed chairs and set them up on the edge of the concrete slab. One boy carried a small brown object which proved to be of interest to several of the kids who were gathering. The item of interest was a portable transistor radio, which magically played music and was not connected to an electrical outlet.

Bobby Darin's voice could be heard singing "Beyond the Sea," a heartthrob of the teen set. Several minutes later, Chubby Checker implored the crowd to get up and dance. Some of the kids arose and started gyrating to the new dance, "The Twist."

Veronica grabbed Teddy and pulled him onto the "dance floor."

Teddy stood there while Veronica twisted.

"All you have to do is pretend you're grinding out a cigarette with your front foot and drying your back with a towel," she told him. Teddy took a few clumsy steps and then sort of got the hang of it, moving to the beat.

"Hey, you're not too bad," Veronica complimented Teddy.

"Too bad? I just need a little practice," he told her.

Presently Roy Orbison began to sing about a pretty woman. The beat was infectious.

"I don't think we can dance the Twist to this one," Veronica said.

A girl with teased hair danced with a nice-looking boy on the basketball court. Right in time with the music she shook her rear end prettily and a couple of the boys watched her.

The boy and girl on the bench turned their backs to the others and began to make out, oblivious to a few comments. The smell of cigarette smoke drifted towards the dancers and Veronica wrinkled her nose.

"Some of the older guys smoke in the woods."

Teddy asked her, "Would you try it?"

"No, the smell makes me sick. How about you?"

"I don't think my mom would want me smoking. But I might just try it sometime."

"Hey! What are you kids doing here? Shouldn't you be in bed by now?" One of the older boys, about fourteen years old, was shouting at Teddy and Veronica.

"Oh leave them alone, Derrick. They're not hurting anyone," a girl told him.

"Yeah but they might see something that's not for children to see," he replied smirking.

Veronica and Teddy turned and began to walk around the side of the church as they heard Little Eva sing her song about The Locomotion. The kids formed a line and gyrated to the music.

"I'll teach you how to do The Locomotion later," Veronica promised Teddy.

"Ok. I guess I'd better go home now."

"All right. Maybe I'll see you tomorrow."

They went their separate ways.

8

THE ACCIDENT

The next evening after dinner Teddy was sitting on the store's front porch waiting for Veronica. When she came out he said, "I have a few nickels. Let's go play the slot machine."

She replied, "Ok but let's wait until Grandma goes into the TV room. Then she won't hear us." Rosie didn't like children playing the machine but sometimes when she was busy they did it anyway.

Feeding the slot machine was easy for the kids. KaChung! Apple, lemon, grapes! KaChung! Banana, grapes, orange! This time the one-armed bandit won and Teddy was left nickel-less. As they were standing in the store, they heard a loud crash and ran out to the store's porch. At the crossroads they could see an older 1950s model car turned on its side in the ditch. Two teenage boys struggled to climb out of the driver's side door but were having trouble opening it.

Teddy and Veronica watched the drama from the porch. They heard Rosie come running down the steps wearing her pink chenille bathrobe and she looked at them and asked, "What happened?"

"I don't know," Veronica told her. "We were going to walk over to the church when we heard this loud noise."

Rosie hurried down the porch steps and over to the car to help the boys open the door. The car door creaked and resisted the effort. Finally, they crawled out and looked at her.

"Are you ok?"

"Yeah I think we are but the car isn't."

"Have you two been drinking?"

"No ma'am. We were just getting ready to turn into the church and then I saw something in the road so I swerved to avoid it and we landed in the ditch."

"What did you see in the road?"

"Well I'm not real sure but it looked like a black cat."

"Uh oh," Rosie groaned. "Do you think you hit it?"

"I don't know."

Since it was almost dark, Rosie asked Veronica to go get the flashlight. The girl ran back in the store to find it.

In the meantime, Rosie looked over at the pathway that led to the dock. She waited, scanning the edges of the road for any sign of what the boys might have hit. The small gray kitten was also observing, and when

Rosie looked toward the dock she saw eyes gleaming in the dark like luminescent pearls. At least one cat was alive, she thought, turning back toward the crash site, dreading what she thought she might find.

Veronica returned with the flashlight and they began shining it on the road and on the edges of the road where the tire tracks had made skid marks.

Soon the light illuminated a heap of black fur on the opposite side of the road from where the car was leaning. There was no movement from the little pile. Veronica started to cry.

9

A KITTEN'S FOLLY

The black kitten was in a playful mood. He had taken a good catnap during the day and he now was full of kitten energy, just looking to create some havoc. A few early lightning bugs made their appearance and he was trying his best to catch every one. The flashing of the little lights was tantalizing and his comical acrobatics would make an Olympic gymnast envious. Executing a perfect airborne pirouette, the kitten caught one of the bugs. He then spit it out because it didn't taste as good as it looked. Under the watchful eye of his mother, the kitten streaked toward the store in a burst of craziness and the older cat ran to keep up with him. She stopped short of the street while her baby continued on toward a group of tiny signal lights. As he reached the middle of the rural intersection, a car came speeding toward him. The driver applied the brakes just a bit too late, hit the black kitten and sent him flying. He landed in the ditch. The car slammed into the ditch on the other side of the road and came to an abrupt stop, with the car leaning on its side. The mama cat, frantic on the roadside, sprinted to her kitten. She cried out but no one paid her any attention. She pawed her baby, trying to bring him back to life. She faintly heard someone sobbing behind her.

By now some people had gathered near the scene. A bit of a commotion was made as the car's driver and passenger were extricated from the mangled steel. Veronica skirted the small group of people and headed toward the two cats. Bending down, she gently picked up the kitten and cradled him in her arms, being careful not to jostle him, in case anything was broken. Unnoticed by anyone, she carried him into the store, followed by the older female cat. Teddy was right by her side, trying to comfort her. The gray kitten had moved onto the store's front porch and waited by the door.

"See if you can find a small box and a towel so I can put him in it," Veronica said to Teddy.

"Do you think he's dead?" he asked.

Veronica put her head down on the kitten's soft chest and listened. She could feel a bit of a vibration but didn't hear any sound.

"I don't know. Let's put him in a box and maybe his mama will come to him."

Teddy went into the back room and returned with a box that had held canned food.

"I couldn't find any towels but we can use my undershirt. Maybe my mom won't notice that it's missing."

"Ok. Let's get him in it and see what his mother will do."

The black one took a shallow breath and tried to focus, looking around at the unfamiliar room. Shelves were stacked with food and in one back corner was a machine with multicolored lights. His mother, now curled around him, licked his head. She continued bathing him as he slowly realized that his back leg hurt. It hurt a lot. He tried to move it but it was too painful. He whimpered and his mother pulled him close to her body. They spent the night in the box. The gray and white kitten slept on a bench on the front porch.

Veronica had bid Teddy goodnight. She then sat down on the floor close to the box, watchful, until Rosie returned and told her to go to bed.

"These cats have to go," Rosie told Veronica the next morning. "The black kitten almost drowned the other day and if I hadn't been up early he would be dead. And now he was hit by the car and will probably be limping the rest of his life. That one is into everything and I'm afraid of what might happen next. He is just a kitten but he creates chaos wherever he goes."

Veronica had taken up her post on the floor beside the box where the cat and kitten had spent the night.

"Maybe in a few days you can see if you can find homes for them," Rosie said to Veronica. "They would be better off if they had owners who would look after them and take care of them."

"But this is their home. Where would they go?"

"I don't know but now they just live on the dock and they're exposed to all kinds of weather. They're not fed regularly and it would just be best to try to find people who want pet cats."

Veronica sighed and gently stroked both cats in the box. She knew her grandmother was right but she didn't like the thought of giving them up, especially since the little black kitten was hurting with a bad leg.

"Could I keep them for just a while longer while the kitten heals? I promise I'll try to find them good homes. Maybe my mom will let me keep one of them."

"You can ask your mother the next time you talk to her."

"Grandma, do you think the kitten's leg is broken?"

Rosie walked over to the box, leaned down and gingerly touched the kitten's hind leg. He tried to withdraw it but it was too painful to move.

"I don't know, sweetie, but it does hurt him. Let's hope he wasn't hurt internally. Go get the cat food and we'll see if he eats some. Then we'll leave them alone for a while."

The mother cat was able to eat a bit of dry food but her kitten just turned his head toward the side of the box. Veronica put some food in a small dish and took it outside to the porch where the gray and white kitten waited.

10

TROPICAL STORM

A few years earlier, at the end of July, 1960, a sultry day over the Mid-Atlantic states was making people miserable. The clouds seemed to hang low as if waiting for a cooling breeze to wipe them away. The humidity was enough to keep most people indoors in front of fans or in the shade of trees outdoors. But even the shade didn't provide much relief to the stifling closeness. Leaves on the trees hung down like damp green laundry.

The storm was wreaking havoc as it passed over the Florida peninsula and on up the east coast. What would be called Tropical Storm Brenda wasn't as devastating as a full blown hurricane but the winds and rain were still deadly. They were able to cause a lot of personal heartache and property damage. Marylanders didn't have much experience dealing with this type of severe weather. Lighthouse Point was somewhat protected from hurricanes, being situated away from the coast. But that didn't mean it was immune to the vagaries of storms.

The wind started to pick up a bit. The graceful drooping branches of the weeping willows began to sway in the breeze.

That day the people of Lighthouse Point went about their regular chores, tending to their gardens, mending nets used in fishing, keeping to their daily schedules. Rosie was stocking food on the shelves of the store, Samuel Gass was painting a fence in the church yard and Andrew was working on his Sunday sermon. The manual typewriter clacked as Andrew put his thoughts and notes on the paper. Besides the typewriter, a chair and a file cabinet, the church had provided him a tiny office space in back of the church. Andrew reflected on how blessed he was for the many good things in his life. He had a loving wife, a job he was thankful for, a group of friends to socialize with and a peaceful part of the state in which to live. He gazed at the Bible that Taffy had donated to the church years ago when they had first come to Lighthouse Point. It was a substantial, leather-bound one with gold engraving on its cover and spine. No one was sure how old it was but the pages were dog-eared and one could tell it had been well-read. He used it each Sunday during worship services.

Carrying it back to the pulpit, he was about to place it on the stand when he noticed something unusual on one of the choir chairs. He walked over to pick it up and saw that the object was a set of false teeth. He chuckled to himself and wondered who the prankster was this time. He took them out to the graveyard and placed them on Stan Teeter's headstone.

"Sometimes I wish you had all your natural teeth when you died," he said to the grave site. Stan didn't answer him.

Andrew and Taffeta had been living in Lighthouse Point for a number of years, enjoying the tiny community. The church members had warmed quickly to the couple, inviting them into their homes and making them feel welcome in a tight-knit community where there were few outsiders who hadn't grown up in the area. The choir had added a few members as Taffeta's warm personality drew in new, musically-inclined folks. She found it easy to communicate with hand gestures and using her talents on the piano, the Methodist church choir was accomplished as much as a small church choir could be. On some Sunday mornings several non-churchgoers in the vicinity even left their windows open to listen to the old familiar hymns sung mightily from the house of God.

After lunch Andrew drove Taffeta to Leonardtown to do some grocery shopping. Every so often she needed to shop at a larger store to buy things that the Lighthouse Point store didn't carry. She depended on Andrew to take her places since she didn't drive a car. Leonardtown was an easy commute from the little crossroads with hardly any traffic on the country roads. On this day with the weather threatening rain, they didn't spend much time in the larger town. Taffeta wanted to surprise Andrew with a special dinner that night.

Arriving back home, Andrew helped carry the groceries into the house and told Taffeta that he was going back to the church to continue working on his sermon. The sky was turning a darker shade of gray as the wind quickened.

Even though Taffeta didn't drive a car, she did know how to take the small fishing boat out by herself. Andrew had taught her how to steer the boat, how to bring it in gently and how to fish and guide it at the same time. She felt a sense of freedom as she maneuvered the boat along the shoreline when she went fishing. She now knew what size fish was acceptable to keep and which ones she had to throw back in the water. She knew where the good holes were to find fish too. Since fishing sometimes tended to be better on the east side of weather fronts, she expected to bring home some fresh fish for their dinner that night. She would fry them and make some coleslaw and hushpuppies, which Andrew loved.

She wrote a quick note and left it on the kitchen table. The note read, "Honey, I'll be back in a little bit. Love you, T". She walked down the gravel and shell pathway to where their boat was tied up, climbed in and pushed it into the water with help from a paddle.

As the boat drifted from the shore, she cranked it and the motor caught and she started steering it toward the open water. Earlier that morning she had bought some bait from Rosie's store and was looking forward to her little excursion. She was proud of the little boat with her name painted on its side.

As she motored out farther from the shoreline, a few drops of rain splattered in the boat's bottom. Taffeta looked up at the sky and was surprised to see how much and how quickly it had become dark, almost like twilight. A strange feeling came over her and she decided to head for home.

The wind-swept water created turbulence that set moored boats rocking along residents' docks. Taffeta's blonde hair started whipping around her face, making it hard for her to see where to steer. The normally placid water began kicking up some small waves, not yet whitecapping but just enough to make the boat rock a bit unsteadily. She tried to get to the life jacket, but it was rarely used and therefore stored where she couldn't reach it while still trying to steer the boat. By now having forgotten about fishing, she was just attempting to bring the boat in from her position in the outer waters. The rain was now coming down in earnest and Taffeta was thoroughly drenched. She thought that the water, which had become her friend over the years was now threatening her very existence. A gust of wind slashed rain sideways, whipping up a frenzy of angry water, too close to her boat. Now she was beginning to panic, thinking about how she was ever going to get back to the safety of her home.

Higher winds and stronger gusts were now tormenting the Potomac River channel. Still fighting the elements, Taffeta was praying for a miracle. Some water sloshed over the side of the boat and the engine sputtered and quit. She looked up at the somber sky and for a moment thought she saw Andrew beckoning to her. Tears appeared on her cheeks but they were indistinguishable from the rain droplets that soaked her face. She wanted to cry out for help, but she knew that no one could hear her even if she had been able to speak. She began to move her lips in prayer, although no sound came from her mouth.

11

AGONY

Andrew removed the last sheet of his sermon from the typewriter and once again read through it, making a few corrections and notes in the margins. This week's lesson was taken from the book of Matthew, chapter 11:28-30: "Come to me, all you are weary and burdened, and I will give you rest. Take my yoke upon you and learn from me, for I am gentle and humble in heart, and you will find rest for your souls. For my yoke is easy and my burden is light." Andrew had prepared what he believed was a good sermon to accompany the Bible passage. His point this Sunday was to have faith in God even though your burdens are heavy. He had compared the faith that a person has when planting crops from small seeds, that flowers and food plants will grow and thrive. He was gathering his things when he glanced out the window to see the storm slashing across the church yard. He grabbed his umbrella and sprinted out to the car, hoping to get home before the weather got worse.

Arriving at home several minutes later, he was surprised to see that the house was dark. It gave him an eerie sensation, and he wondered why Taffeta hadn't turned on the lights when the sky became so dark. It was unusual for her to lie down in the daytime, he thought, but perhaps she had decided to take a nap. As he walked into the kitchen and turned on the overhead light, he saw Taffeta's note she had left for him. Reading it, he wondered where she might have gone and why she hadn't come back yet. He saw that there were no signs of dinner. The storm was intensifying and he began to worry about her, thinking she might have been caught in it. He looked around the house, calling her name. Taffeta didn't answer him.

He reassured himself that she must have gone to a neighbor's house and decided to wait out the storm there. He had lost track of time while writing his sermon, but he suddenly felt hungry and realized that it was past dinner time. He made himself a sandwich and washed it down with some tea. As it grew later he decided that he needed to look for Taffeta. All this was so unlike her and he now had an uneasy feeling about the situation. Where was she? Had something happened to her? A sense of foreboding came over him. Then he stopped and tried to think rationally. Nothing had happened; she was just someplace waiting until the storm passed.

Andrew picked up the phone to call his nearest neighbor, but the phone was dead. So he went into the living room and tried to read a book but was distracted and gave up. Andrew got up and looked out the window at the rain, which by now was gale-force. What to do? He found a flashlight in a drawer and shined it out several windows but all he could see was the fierce rain and the trees that were nearly bent to the ground. This was the worst storm he had seen since their move to Lighthouse Point. He felt a bit queasy. Just as a hunch he thought he should check on the boat to see how it was faring in the storm. He put on a raincoat and hat and carrying his flashlight, he fought the storm down the pathway. Almost blown away in the sixty mile an hour winds, he came to the end of the walkway and discovered the boat was gone! There was no sign of it anywhere. Had it become unmoored and drifted away? Then a terrible thought came to him. Surely Taffeta was not out in it!

"Oh God!" he cried. He didn't know what to do next. "Oh, please, no! NO!"

He ran back to the house and tried to compose himself but was unsuccessful. He tried to reason that Taffy hadn't actually taken the boat out in this storm, but had a sick feeling that she did. Overcome with fear and anxiety, he had to do something. But what could he do? Slamming the door behind him, he went running out into the road shouting Taffy's name over and over. The wind blew his words away.

Andrew ran down the road to the store, slipping in the mud puddles. He could see a faint light in the upstairs window that indicated Rosie was still awake. Pounding on the door, and soaked to the bone, he waited impatiently as Rosie made her way down the stairs to let him in.

His wild eyes showing his fear, he stepped inside as Rosie took in the scene.

"She's gone! Taffy's gone!"

"What? Where is she, Andrew?" Rosie asked gently.

"I don't know but the boat's gone!" As he stood there dripping, Rosie stepped back to grip the counter.

"Do you know for sure that she took the boat out? Maybe it just blew away in the storm."

"No, I don't think so," he replied.

"Oh my stars! I sold her some bait earlier today! I never thought she was planning to go out in the boat on her own!"

Andrew looked at her, his face pale. "She's out there in the boat, alone in this storm!" He grabbed the side of the counter and looked like he was going to collapse so Rosie led him to a chair and he sank down in it.

"She must have decided to go fishing. She said she was going to fix you a special dinner tonight."

"What can we do? How can we find her?" he demanded.

Rosie, near tears, touched his arm. "Andrew, I'm sorry, but it's so bad out there I don't think any of the watermen can risk going out right now. Let me go out to ring the bell," she told him.

He just sat there looking dazed and put his hand over his eyes as if trying to shield them from the truth.

Rosie put on a raincoat and went to the front door. When she opened it, the wind nearly blew her backwards and it was all she could do to close it behind her. She lowered her head and fought her way out to the front yard where an old dinner bell was attached to a post. The dinner bell was only used in an extreme emergency to call the men of the community together. Still trying to stay on her feet as the wind tried to knock her down, she pulled on the rope attached to the bell over and over. The bell tolled a sad bong, bong. Bong, bong. Rarely used, the bell was rusting at its edges but still was able to produce the sonorous sound that put knots in people's stomachs. The ringing bell always foretold of a tragedy.

Rosie staggered back to the store, pushed by the winds. Just as she was opening the door she heard a tremendous crash. A sound like splintering wood pierced the sodden air. She glanced around the side of the store just in time to see the old house behind the store come apart in the wind. Pieces of wood siding were flying helter-skelter. A window broke loose from its casing and went tumbling end on end down the path toward the water. Sand, mixed with the rain, pelted Rosie, stinging her face. Quickly taking shelter in the store, Rosie was barely able to shut the door behind her. Andrew sat staring vacantly, oblivious to all the noise and destruction. She was praying the old store would hold up and not be blown away like the house. There was no storm cellar for them to go to. The wind rattled the windows and shook the building.

Rosie didn't want to upset Andrew any more than he already was, so she said nothing. Walking around to the back, she looked through the window that faced the old house next door. She was startled to see the house had blown off its foundation. Even though she had seen parts of it blowing past her, she hadn't realized that the whole house was gone. All that was left were a few pieces of broken wood. She knew there had been furniture inside the house, but it was all broken or blown away. In the dark, Rosie could still see enough to recognize debris flying through the air. The willow trees in the yard were draped across the ground like tattered ribbons in the rampaging storm. She had no experience with tornados, but knew that this must be one.

Luckily, no one had lived in that old house for years. The owners had moved out and left some items that they hadn't needed. No one had been interested in buying the house since then. She prayed that none of the occupied houses in town had suffered the same fate.

The storm continued to rage outside and all Rosie could do was wait, and watch over the stricken Andrew. In the dark Rosie felt her way to the counter and rummaged under it for the flashlight. She wanted to get behind the stairwell for protection. As she turned on the flashlight and moved toward Andrew, she thought she heard someone banging on the door. She hesitated, thinking that surely no one was out in this storm, but then the banging came again. When she opened the door, she saw a figure bundled up in a yellow raincoat with a hood, hunched over against the wind. Rosie opened the door and Samuel Gass almost blew into the store. Dripping rain on the floor, he removed his hood and immediately saw Andrew on the chair staring at the floor as if in a trance.

"What is it, Rosie? What happened?"

"Andrew said that Taffy is missing. He said the boat is gone too."

"Uh oh." He walked over to Andrew and put his hand on the other man's shoulder. Andrew started shaking slightly and buried his face in his hands.

"Take me out to look for her!" Andrew pleaded.

Samuel stooped down so he was eye level with the distraught minister and gently responded, "No, we can't right now. It looks like a small tornado just passed through here and we can't put any men in boats on the water until the storm passes. Are you sure that Taffy is out in the boat?"

"The boat's gone and so is Taffy!" he cried in anguish. "Where else could she be?"

"Rosie, do you have anything strong to drink?" Samuel asked.

"Uh, yeah. Let me go upstairs to get something," The flashlight shone ahead of her as she went up the stairs, leaving the men in the dark. They were silent as each were deep in their own troubled thoughts.

As Rosie came back down the steps carrying a bottle and two glasses, Samuel said, "We'll get a group together first thing in the morning to go out to search for her. All we can do now is try to be strong and pray."

Rosie poured two glasses of gin straight from the bottle and handed them to the men. Sipping the alcohol, the awful reality of the situation began to set in among the friends.

12

THE GREEN BOAT

The destruction was worse than anything the community had ever seen. The mini tornado had only touched down here and there, skipping over one home while taking the chimney or porch off the next. Strong straight line winds had uprooted trees, a few of which fell onto the roof of a frightened family. The unfortunate ones who experienced more of the storm's wrath were helped by those who had been luckier. The store was still intact, and the Methodist Church building was fine, even though a couple of headstones in the graveyard had been knocked over. The day dawned brightly, such a bold contrast to the horror of the previous night. Puddles of water were strewn across the roads, making it impossible for cars or people to cross. Most areas were low-lying, and the water was slow in seeping into the ground. As soon as it was safe, Samuel rounded up a group of watermen who launched their boats in the murky water to begin the search for Taffeta. Debris littered the shoreline, washed up from miles away. Objects that didn't belong in water surfaced, like a child's toy truck and a torn plastic lawn chair. People who lived on the waterfront watched as the boats motored out and began to slowly scan the surface for Andrew's boat. The most bizarre thing discovered was a car door wrapped around the middle of an oak tree.

To the relief of everyone in town, the electricity flickered a few times and then came back on. Rosie made a big pot of coffee for anyone who stopped by to talk about the storm. Word had already spread about the missing Taffy, and men spoke in hushed voices as they entered the store to respond to the bell's call for help. A feeling of gloom permeated the community. While some tried to keep their hopes up, the townfolk had a history of knowing what tragedies could unfold in angry seas. They were facing the fact that they had lost someone new, but someone they had taken into their hearts. Her cheerful and upbeat nature had endeared Taffy to the members of the community, even beyond Andrew's congregation.

Samuel took Andrew with him in his fishing boat. Neither had slept at all and both were exhausted, mentally and emotionally. Andrew looked beaten but he determinedly searched the water for any sign of Taffy. He had offered up so many prayers he wondered whether God was still listening to him. His eyes were bleary and his knuckles were as white as his haggard face.

After hours of finding nothing but rubble, some of the men puttered in and met at the store. Rosie had made them some sandwiches, which were devoured quickly. As this was a Sunday, church services had been called off. Andrew hadn't even thought about opening the church; he was only focused on finding Taffy. Hopes dimmed as the day wore on.

Around dinner time, an older boat was seen heading toward the dock, towing something behind it. A few people ran out to the end of the dock to find out if there was any news. The closer the boat came to the water's edge, the more the object being towed looked like Andrew's boat, "Taffy." The green painted sides signaled the certainty that it was indeed his boat. Battered and a bit splintered, the "Taffy" looked forlorn and oh so empty. The man towing the boat said that he found it just around the point, where once a person could look out at an island and see the old lighthouse. Several years previously vandals burned the lighthouse down and it was now in ruins, as the green boat would surely become in the future.

Andrew and Samuel had decided to take a break for a few hours to try to get some sleep before resuming their search. Exhausted as they both were, sleep didn't come easily to either man. A church member reluctantly walked down the lane to rouse Samuel and Andrew to break the bad news. Approaching Samuel's house first, he could see him through the window, staring out at the road. Slowly the door opened and

Samuel questioned the visitor silently. The man just sadly shook his head. Resigned, they both walked toward Andrew's cottage, dreading the next few minutes.

Andrew was fitfully sleeping on the wicker couch on his back porch. The two men walked through Andrew's front door, which was left unlocked, like all the other homes in town. Not wanting to startle him, Samuel gently called from the bedroom doorway. "Andy, we've come to talk to you." He was instantly awake, sitting up on the couch, and asked, "Have you found her?"

"Andy, your boat was found but they didn't find Taffy. Jim Calvert, here, towed it in, and it's down near the dock."

Silence.

"She's gone, isn't she?"

"We don't know for sure but the men will keep looking for her tomorrow as soon as it gets light," Samuel tried to reassure him.

More silence.

Pulling himself up, Andrew told them, "Well I guess I'll go down to see the boat."

Trudging toward the dock, the three men didn't say much, each engrossed in their own thoughts. Approaching the dock, they could see that Jim had pulled the green fishing boat up on the shore. The boat's name, "Taffy" was plainly in sight. Some people remained in the area, offering words of condolence to Andrew as he passed. He squared his shoulders as if taking on a mighty burden and placed his hands on the letters he had painted years ago, running his fingers over them again and again.

Someone started crying at the end of the dock.

13

HIALEAH

Taffy never did surface, even though a great effort was made to find her. Andrew grew depressed, ate little, and stayed in his house, away from the other residents of the community. Ladies from the Methodist Church brought casseroles each day and left them in the refrigerator, where they remained, ignored and uneaten. Finally, after a week, Samuel had a talk with Andrew.

"Andy, some of us have been talking and we think you should have a memorial service for Taffy. We can get Reverend Wright to do it and we can buy a headstone to put up in the church cemetery if you wish. It might help to have a ceremony to honor her life. You know how important rituals are to people. What do you think?"

"I don't know. Let me think about it."

"Do you have any family you'd like to invite if you decide to have a service?"

"Just a niece of Taffy's who lives in Virginia. Her parents and older sister are deceased so I don't know of anyone else. Hialeah is her name and I think she's about twenty-five years old now."

"Well, let me know what you want to do. I'll help you any way I can."

Reverend Wright visited with Andrew the next day and he counseled the younger man. Andrew found some comfort in discussing his grief with him, even though he felt overwhelmed by everything that had happened. He kept losing his train of thought and would stop in mid-sentence and try to remember the point of his idea. They decided to have the service the following week. Reverend Wright asked many questions about Taffy's life and Andrew choked up when talking about her. He recalled many of the times they had together and tried to focus on his wife's beautiful smile, her sweet demeanor and his enduring love for her even if she was no longer with him. Depression had set in during the short time since Taffy had drowned. Andrew knew he should try harder to look like he was coping but found it almost impossible. He had experienced one of his terrible headaches and he had lost weight. He found Hialeah's phone number and called her to tell her about the memorial service. Hialeah was shocked and saddened to hear the news but said she'd be there the next week. The two had never met but he was curious about seeing Taffy's only living relative.

The week dragged on and Andrew found himself counting the days until the service. He had taken a leave from the church for a few weeks and now he realized he had time on his hands. He wandered around the house, not eating much and not sleeping much. He didn't know what to do with himself so he pulled out some old photographs that were in an album and flipped through them. A photo of Taffy on a park bench in Georgetown. One of their old DeSoto. More pictures of places they used to frequent when they lived in Washington. Another one of them together holding hands as they stood in front of the Washington Monument. Whoever had taken the picture had cut off the top half of the monument but that didn't matter. A more recent one of Taffy holding a string of fish she had caught created a sick feeling in his stomach. He removed that one and tucked it underneath some others. He was not only extremely sad but was also lonely. He missed her so much it physically hurt. How was he going to go on living without her? His faith in God was about the only thing that had kept him sane. Every day he asked God, "Why? Why my Taffy?" He sought answers to questions that had no answers.

The day of the memorial service was hot. August in Southern Maryland could be stifling and this day exemplified the dog days of summer. Eleven o'clock was the time and the place was the church. People dressed in dark colors crowded into the pews and started fanning themselves with paper fans. Some of the women blotted their faces delicately with handkerchiefs. A substitute piano player warmed up with a few favorite old hymns. More people came and found there were no seats left so they either stood in the back or just waited outside the front of the church. Everyone wanted to pay their respects to Andrew as he was well-liked throughout Lighthouse Point.

The front row had been reserved for Andrew and Hialeah. As she walked in, several people turned their heads and exclaimed how much she resembled Taffy. Her long blonde hair flowed around her shoulders and her features were strikingly similar to Taffy's. There was no mistaking that the two had come from the same family. As she was guided down the aisle toward the front pew, someone sitting behind Andrew gasped softly at the resemblance and Andrew turned around. He was astounded when he saw Hialeah, who had the same green eyes as Taffy's, the same hair and build. She was a younger version of his beloved Taffy. She sat down beside him and he grasped her hand.

"I'm so glad you could come," he said. "I'm Andrew."

"I'm so sorry that we had to meet under these circumstances," she responded. "I wish I had visited you and Aunt Taffy before the accident."

About that time the service began with the hymn, <u>O God, Our Hope in Ages Past.</u> Everyone rose to sing in unison. During the service Andrew was barely able to give the homily, which was very difficult for him but he knew that Taffy would have liked it. There was a reception in the choir room following the service with so many people trying to pay their respects that the line stretched out the door and into the parking lot.

Afterward Hialeah had to return home but she promised Andrew she would visit him soon. The mourners had gone home and Andrew resignedly began the walk home to an empty house.

He wrote in his diary that night:

> *Dear Diary,*
>
> *This was one of the saddest days of my life. It was as painful as when I realized that she was missing, but then I clung to the hope that there had been a mistake, and that somehow she would walk through the door again. Thinking of her out in the boat made me think of my father falling off the bridge into the water, not being able to make it to shore. The only day that was harder than today was when I realized that she really wasn't coming back. Thank God I was able to get through it. I am so blessed to have friends here who have supported me during these terrible days.*

I'm so glad Hialeah was able to come to the service. Taffy and I really don't have any other family besides her. I pray for comfort and healing of my broken heart. My headache is killing me so I must try to sleep now.

14

ANDREW'S FATHER

Ever since he was a boy, Andrew had kept a diary or journal of some sort. He began writing about his activities when he was thirteen years old, after a catastrophe hit his family. Years before, when he was just a little child, his mother had passed away from a mysterious malady that no one ever discussed with him. Since he was so young, he didn't have much recollection of her; just a few items that had been her personal possessions were now his property. Her brush and comb set, a hand-crafted jewelry box and a small collection of old hats were stored away in his bedroom closet. His father had several black and white pictures of her that he kept on the mantel of the fireplace. Andrew had memorized her features over the years and found himself resembling her more and more as he grew up. She had been an attractive woman with dark wavy hair and an intelligent face. She was smiling at the photographer as if she was hiding a secret. Years later Andrew, browsing through an art history text in the high school library, was surprised to find that the Mona Lisa had a similar expression and was described as having a secret. At times, he would ask his father what had happened to his mother but the only answers he got were unsatisfactory. He said, "She was very sick and then God decided to take her home." Or "I loved her very much, but she was always frail and her time had come." These responses didn't really satisfy Andrew, but he knew not to press his father too much. Only one time did he pursue his questioning, and asked, "But what did she die from?" His father's face crumpled, and he rushed from the room. Andrew never asked again.

They both continued to live in the old house, built in the early part of the century, in a pleasant neighborhood in Northern Virginia. Andrew did well in school and liked sports. He wished he had a mother in his life or even a female to look after him, but the only close relative who lived nearby was Aunt Martha, who was his father's sister. She was a tall woman with dark, piercing eyes. Andrew felt that she looked at him with complete indifference, with no concern for him or his thoughts. This was completely unlike the gaze of his father, which always made him feel safe and comfortable. It was apparent that she had been attractive when she was younger but her beauty had faded over the years. He didn't really care much for Aunt Martha and had the feeling she didn't care much for him either. She was always cordial enough when they saw each other, but presented somewhat of a distant attitude that didn't endear her to Andrew. She remembered his birthdays and at Christmas time but didn't make much of an effort to be present in his life as he matured.

One day while he was studying history in his class, a lady who worked in the principal's office came in and spoke with the teacher. Andrew thought he was in trouble when the teacher slowly approached his desk and, with a serious voice, said, "Andrew, you need to close your book and go with Miss Jenkins." Andrew was perplexed but did what he was told. As they walked toward the principal's office, Miss Jenkins said, "Mr. Shaw needs to talk with you." Her voice was very kind, so perhaps whatever he was being sent to the principal for wasn't too serious.

"Andrew, please have a seat," Mr. Shaw told him. Andrew sat on the worn loveseat and stared at the principal. Mr. Shaw was on the heavy side and he wore a bow tie that was a bit crooked. He was almost totally bald and the few hairs he had left straggled solemnly around his ears. He came around the side of his desk and sat down beside Andrew. "Son, there's been a bad accident. Your father was working on the bridge and, well, uh, Andrew, your dad is gone. He died this morning."

Andrew sat in his seat, stunned. His hand tightened on the armrest. He knew his father had a job

LINDA C MARCHMAN

working on the new Memorial Bridge that spanned the Potomac River that led into Washington. Mr. Shaw put his arm around Andrew's shoulders and told him how sorry he was. A tear trickled down Andrew's cheek as the terrible news penetrated his mind. His father was dead. He didn't have a father anymore. He didn't have a mother either, so......what would happen to him now? He buried his head in his hands and cried silently in his shock. What would he do and how would he live without any parents? So many questions and no answers.

"What happened to my father?"

"He accidentally fell into the water and wasn't able to swim to safety. He drowned in the river."

Mr. Shaw gently pulled him closer and hugged him. "We didn't know who your next of kin was, but we found out from your school records that you have an aunt who lives close by. She is listed here as Martha O'Connor, your father's only sister. Is that right?"

"Yes, Aunt Martha. She lives in Alexandria."

"I don't know if she's aware of what happened to your father, but she'll find out soon enough."

Andrew couldn't move and could barely breathe. His head felt like it was underwater and he shook it slightly to clear it. The image of his father drowning in the Potomac River almost made him physically sick, but he held on to the loveseat and gazed down at the floor.

"Are you all right?" Mr. Shaw asked him.

"I think so. Well, maybe not," was the reply.

Mr. Shaw patted Andrew's arm. "Here, let me get you a drink of water. Just try to take it easy for a while." Andrew watched as his principal glided out of the office.

15

ALEXANDRIA

A couple of days passed. The shock of losing his father had not worn off and Andrew was thrust into a new situation and a new home. His belongings had been gathered from the school and he had been taken to Aunt Martha's house. In a short time, it was determined that eventually Andrew's house would have to be sold and he would live permanently with Aunt Martha. He would have to leave his school and everyone he had known since first grade. Andrew drifted through the days, not really believing what was happening and hoping what he dreaded would not come to pass. The thought of staying with his aunt was not pleasant, but there really was no other place he could go. The thought dawned on him that he was an orphan. Orphans usually lived in a big building with other orphans. This thought made him uneasy. It might be just like Aunt Martha to decide she really didn't want him living in her house and send him to the home for orphans.

The funeral was a blur. Many of his father's friends from work attended the service and afterward, expressed their sympathies to Andrew and Martha. The boy didn't really remember much of what went on, but the biggest thing that made an impression on him was the gray casket that held the remains of his father's body that was wheeled into the church and parked in the front, just four feet from where Andrew sat with his aunt. He imagined that this was all just a joke, that his father would open the top of the casket, sit up, look around and gaze at him. Of course, that didn't happen and slowly Andrew faced the truth that his father wasn't coming back and that he would not see him again.

They buried Michael Maye in an old cemetery in Alexandria, beside his wife. The cemetery was located on one of the "royalty" streets, so named for people whose titles didn't exist in the United States...King, Queen, Prince, Duke, etc. As the mourners stood outside, listening to the preacher say a few words of comfort, the sky opened up with a deluge of cold rain. No one had expected it to rain so most people went scurrying to take shelter. Aunt Martha took Andrew by the arm and led him away from the gravesite. Andrew took one long, last look at the great hole in the ground where the casket would be lowered. The rain made rivulets of clay run into the freshly-excavated chasm. As they sloshed their way back home, Andrew looked up through the fog and rain to see the majestic Masonic Temple dispassionately perched on its hill, overlooking the proceedings.

That night, he found a writing tablet and pencil and began recording his thoughts that would become his diary.

>*My dad died in an accident while he was working. We had his funeral today and he was buried beside my mother. I have moved in with Aunt Martha, but I hope it's just for a little while. They are going to sell my house so I won't be going back to live there anymore. I might not see my friends either. I have a small room upstairs that Aunt Martha says is now mine. It's not as big as my old bedroom was, but there's a little window I can look out to see the street. I think it was a storage room before I moved in. I'm sleeping on a cot. I will have to go to another school next week.*

16

AUNT MARTHA

Aunt Martha lived in a brick house that had a small front yard enclosed with a wrought iron fence. The house itself was three stories tall, built of old red brick and was squeezed in beside two other similar houses. Its neighborhood was neat but not ritzy. It was a comfortable place but the interior exuded an aura of neglect. There were no photographs on the tables or walls. The furniture was spare but did include some antiques. Doilies adorned the arms and backs of wing chairs. A dusty grand piano in one corner of the living room hadn't been played in many years. Andrew's room was on the third floor, away from the other bedrooms. It held a cot and a dresser. There was a small writing desk and a window where he could watch the happenings on the street.

Andrew walked the historic streets to his new school the following week. He passed by some cobblestone streets that had been in use for over 150 years. He imagined how it would feel riding his bike on the bumpy stones. That made him sad because he thought he might not be able to have his bike now that he had moved in with Aunt Martha. It turned out that Andrew actually could never ride his bike again. He didn't know what happened to it, but assumed it was given away.

Aunt Martha had enrolled him a few days earlier in school and now he was on his way to this different place, a place he didn't want to be. He reluctantly approached the big brick school, and his steps faltered as he saw a lot of kids milling around the front entrance. Many were in groups, talking and laughing. He walked slowly up to them and they ignored him like he was invisible. Laughing and whispering, a group of girls crowded around in a circle. Looking around, he didn't see anyone he knew of course, so he just kept his eyes on the ground and shuffled his feet, waiting for the bell to ring.

Brrrinnng! The students started moving toward the double doors like a big wave at the beach that starts crashing toward the shoreline. A bit of pushing and mild shoving allowed them to squeeze through the portals and begin to disperse toward their classrooms. Andrew stood in the lobby, looking like a lost puppy in an unfamiliar room. Another wave of students swept past him as he finally saw a sign over a door to his left that read, "Office." Avoiding some last minute stragglers, he maneuvered his way through the door and went up to the counter. An older lady with graying hair and a round face sat behind a typewriter and looked up at him, asking, "What can I do for you, young man?"

Andrew sort of stammered and said, "Well, uh, I'm new here and I don't know where I should go."

"What's your name?"

"Andrew Maye."

She sorted through a stack of papers on her desk while Andrew waited. "Oh, ok. Martha O'Connor was here last week and said you'd be starting school this morning." She read through one paper and glanced up at Andrew. "I'm sorry about your father. What a tragedy." He just stared at her. It hadn't occurred to him that strangers would know about his life. Then he remembered his manners and thanked her.

"I hope you'll like it here. You had good grades at your other school, so we've placed you in appropriate classes so you'll be able to work up to your full potential."

"Yes, Ma'am."

"I'm going to assign you a locker for your books and then we'll get you into your first period class." Andrew watched as she heaved herself up from the chair and opened a file drawer. She fumbled through some locks, withdrew one and handed it to him. She then had him sign a paper that certified he was checking out that particular lock and he kept another paper with numbers of his combination printed on it. She also gave him a sheet of paper with his schedule.

"Ok, you'll go all the way down the hall to your right and it will be the last door on the left, room 126. Mr. Farmer is your math teacher. He'll check out a book for you."

"Thank you," Andrew said again and turned to leave the office.

"Oh, by the way, Martha is a friend of mine, so I'll be able to report to her about your progress."

17

PAIN

The first attack came during Mr. Farmer's class. Andrew was sitting quietly at his desk working on a math problem when all of a sudden his head felt like it was exploding. He put both hands on either side of his head to try to make the pain stop. But it didn't. He massaged his temples but the pain increased. He started feeling disoriented and thought he was going to faint. Putting his head down on his desk, Andrew closed his eyes and prayed the pain would go away. Mr. Farmer noticed his new student was in difficulty and walked down the aisle to see what was wrong. Touching Andrew on the shoulder he asked, "Son, are you okay?"

Through the pain Andrew winced and thickly said, "No, I don't think so."

"Do you want to go to the clinic?"

"No, just let me rest for a minute."

Some of the other students were staring at him, but he didn't notice. For the rest of the class, he didn't move his head off the desk. The throbbing was almost unbearable. At the sound of the bell, he told Mr. Farmer he thought he should go home.

Just walking down the hall to the office took a great effort. He tried to concentrate on putting one foot in front of the other as he slowly made his way toward the front of the school. As he opened the office door, he saw the office lady watching him.

"I think I need to go home. I'm not feeling well."

"You certainly don't look well. Can I get in touch with your aunt somehow?"

"No, I don't think she's home. It's not far; I can walk back."

"You're very pale. I think you should wait here until I can get Martha to come get you."

It was an effort just trying to talk and Andrew didn't mean to be rude, but he felt like he had to get out of this school.

"I have to go now. I'll be okay," and he turned and walked out of his new school. He hadn't even been there two hours.

He stumbled down the sidewalk and headed in the direction of Aunt Martha's house. The bright sunlight glared in his eyes, almost blinding him. He tried to walk in the shade of the old trees and that helped a bit. He sat down on a bench to rest and leaned forward to hold his head up with a hand. Time passed and he wasn't aware of how long he had been sitting, trying to muster the strength to continue down the street. People who passed by glanced at him, probably wondering why the boy was not in school. Not taking any notice of the cobblestone streets or the pedestrians, he slowly threaded his way to his new home and his tiny bedroom.

A few hours later Aunt Martha came home and saw Andrew's books on the table. Surely he shouldn't be home from school so soon, but she couldn't believe that he had forgotten them on his first day of classes. She climbed the stairs and walked into his room where he was fast asleep on the cot. She just stood there in mild confusion wondering why he was home so early.

"Andrew! Why aren't you in school?" she demanded.

Just barely awake, he responded, "I'm sick."

"What's wrong with you?" she asked impatiently.

"My head hurts."

She looked at him closer and could see that he really was suffering. Her tone changed a bit as she asked him if he wanted something to drink.

"No. I just need to rest."

"Maybe I should get the doctor."

"No, I hope that the pain will just go away."

So she closed the door and went back down the stairs and left him in his misery. As she sat at her kitchen table, she reflected on Andrew's illness. Just like his mother, she thought to herself. Martha hoped that she hadn't taken on too much of a burden when she took in her nephew. She didn't know how to help him and she just hoped that this was an isolated incident. Maybe all the events of the past few weeks were just affecting him now and hopefully he would snap out of it soon.

18

ADJUSTMENT

As the weeks dragged on, Andrew found it difficult adjusting to his new circumstances. Every morning he got up and walked to the new school but didn't make any friends. He became known as "the new boy who has headaches." The headaches occurred about once a week and completely disabled him. He either staggered back to Aunt Martha's house or would just wait it out in the back room of the office. Nothing seemed to help relieve the pain except time. He had always been healthy, participating in sports and had belonged to a group of friends at his old school. Now his life had turned upside down and he felt depressed. There was not much he could do to relieve the headaches and was afraid to try new things for fear he would be laughed at. Most of the other students just ignored him as he sidled his way through his classes. It was almost like he was invisible as he drifted through the hallways, not acknowledging anyone. He faded into the background like a shade of beige against a white wall.

Andrew's grades began to drop and the principal was notified. Mr. Patterson was a tall, kindly man who wore dark suits every day along with gold rimmed glasses perched on the end of his nose. He called Andrew into his office and gestured toward a chair facing his desk.

Andrew squirmed a bit under the gaze of Mr. Patterson but was put at ease as they began to talk.

"Andrew, some of your teachers have reported that your grades aren't the best. Is there something we can do to help you?"

"I get these headaches and I can't concentrate on my work," he replied.

"Have you been to see a doctor?"

"No sir."

Mr. Patterson regarded Andrew for a minute. "I know what happened to your father and I'm truly sorry. I know that Martha took you in because your mother is also deceased. I realize that losing your father, moving in with a relative, and starting at a new school is a lot to handle. It's no wonder that you haven't kept up the grades that you had at your previous school. I just want you to know if there's ever anything you want to discuss, please come to me."

"Thank you, sir."

"I hope that time will heal some of your heartache. You've been through a very hard time and I intend to keep you in my sight. In the meantime, I want you to try to make friends with some of the other boys. Talk to them. See if you have anything in common. Even one or two friends will be good for you."

"I'll try, sir."

"I know your Aunt Martha can be difficult but you'll just have to put up with her until you're older. See if you can find something that would make her happy and then she wouldn't think of you as a burden but as an asset."

Andrew thought about this and said, "Maybe I can get a part time job and bring home some money. That would make her happy."

"That might be a good thing for both of you."

As Andrew left the office he started thinking about where he could find a job and bring up his grades.

The headaches continued but Andrew found he could somewhat manage them if he went right to bed when his head first started hurting. He kept busy with his schoolwork and his new part time job he found as an errand and delivery boy for a corner grocery store in downtown Alexandria. The job didn't pay much, but he also collected tips from the ladies on his delivery route. The money he made went to Aunt Martha who told him she was saving money for his college education. He sometimes wondered about the truth when he saw she had bought herself another new dress but he didn't question her. His aunt used him to run her errands and do housework.

His life plodded along as he adjusted to his tiny third floor room and his somewhat insignificant role as a guest in Aunt Martha's house. An interest in history made itself evident as he began to take notice of his surroundings in historic Alexandria. He marveled at the architecture of the old buildings and houses. In his free time, he took long walks around the neighborhoods that had been populated by the important people of centuries past. Andrew could imagine that he was actually walking the same streets as George Washington did in the late 1700s. He began to appreciate the fact that he lived in such an historic place and determined that he would make the best of it for the next few years he had to live there. He wasn't aware that his mother had also walked the same streets years ago, admiring the same buildings. Andrew acquired a used fishing pole and would walk down to the waterfront to try to catch some fish from the Potomac River. If he caught a decent-sized one, he would bring it home, clean it and present it to his aunt to be cooked for dinner. Since he proved to be a good worker and was bringing home some extra money, Martha's attitude toward him eased a bit. She no longer thought of him as an albatross around her neck, but as a young person who could be useful to her. She couldn't admit that she loved the boy, but she seemed to tolerate him and his headaches in a slightly more compassionate way.

19

WAR

Andrew had graduated from high school and was looking for a job, hopefully somewhere close to Alexandria since Aunt Martha now was not in the best of health. She needed him to do more and more for her as she wasn't physically able to keep her house in shape or even do her own shopping anymore. She had gained weight because she was unable to get around, and that had in turn made her arthritis more painful. She had given up hope of ever marrying again. Actually, she was still married to Charles O'Connor. He had disappeared years ago and had stopped sending her money. She had no idea where he had gone, and it didn't really matter. He was never going to come back. Anyway, she had Andrew to depend on now. He was her only living relative. For his part, Andrew still found her difficult to live with. But she was kinder than she had been originally. He knew that she was in pain, and he could ignore the occasional verbal stings. He felt a responsibility toward her as his aunt since she had given him a home when he became an orphan. He determined that he would do his best to keep her as comfortable as he could.

The war was heating up and many young men his age were enlisting in the service. Since Aunt Martha was not bound to live much longer, much less support herself, he didn't have the choice of enlisting. He had to stay home, and find a job that would support them both. He felt no resentment toward her; he was grateful to be young with many possibilities ahead of him.

Finally, he was able to procure a job at the nearby Naval Torpedo Station, helping to produce munitions for the war. He also joined the plant bowling league where he met other young people engaged in the same work pursuits. Taking care of Aunt Martha took up much of his spare time so he didn't participate in many other outside activities.

He wrote in his journal,

> *I'm lucky that things have worked out for me the past few years. I'm still living with Aunt Martha, which isn't ideal, but having a good job right here in Alexandria has helped. I feel like I am contributing to the war effort even though I wasn't able to enlist. Many men my age have left to serve our country to fight our enemies and I keep abreast of all the*

new developments by reading the Washington Post. I have conflicting feelings about the war. I'm basically a pacifist but I don't see much choice these days but to get involved in our patriotic effort to suppress the tyrants. I just hope the war doesn't drag on for years and that our troops will return safely at its conclusion.

My social life isn't the greatest but I'm pretty busy working and taking care of Aunt Martha. I would like to go to college one day. I don't know yet what I'd like to study. But for now I must keep working so we can stay in her house and have a decent roof over our heads. I pray that God will watch over us and keep Aunt Martha as free of pain as possible.

20

THE EARLY YEARS

S ome years before Andrew moved in with her, his Aunt Martha had been married to a salesman. Martha was an attractive, strong-willed, dark-haired young woman who had several suitors before she caught the eye of Charles O'Connor. Charles typified a happy-go-lucky Irishman. He enjoyed life and was known to tip a glass or two, but not to excess. He was originally from Chicago but had recently moved to Alexandria. After a short engagement, Charles and Martha were married in Alexandria and began their life together. It was a disaster from the beginning. Charles was gone each week, working at his sales job, which upset Martha. He would come home on Friday, after being away, looking tired.

"Charles, I was wondering when you were coming home. I thought you were going to get back earlier."

"Martha, I've told you I'm a salesman and most of what I do is traveling and selling. I have to make money to keep up our place here and put food on our table. So what do you want me to do?"

"Well I just wish we could spend more time together. It gets lonely staying home all day, with nothing to do."

"Why don't you find something to do? What do your other friends do during the day?"

"Some of them have children, so that keeps them busy."

Charles said, "We've already talked about having children and you know what we decided."

"I'm not ready for any children. I don't even like the thought of having any!"

"And we're not in any financial position to have any, even if we wanted them."

"I just wish we had more money and then things would be better."

"Better, how? I'd still be traveling and you'd still be sitting at home, bored."

"I'm just not the type to take care of babies, changing diapers and doing all that stuff. I didn't even like babysitting for the neighbors when I was a teenager."

"Right now, I'd like to eat dinner and then relax for a while, if you don't mind." He fixed himself a drink and went to the living room to avoid further arguing.

Martha sighed and moved away and took her place at the counter in the kitchen where she had been preparing the food. She was perturbed with Charles, but she knew there was not much that she could do to remedy the situation.

The same conversation occurred almost every Friday night, with slight variation, when Charles would return home from work. Martha was frustrated with her lack of direction and Charles was just trying to make a living. He felt unappreciated and thought that Martha should be more grateful that he even had a job, at a time when jobs like his were hard to come by.

The arguments continued along the same lines, with Martha wanting her life to be better in some un-specified way, and Charles having no idea what could possibly satisfy her. He just wished she would say that she was glad he was home, and that they could have a pleasant dinner table conversation about the news or sports.

One week Charles told Martha that he wouldn't be home that weekend. One could see the anger creeping across her face as she tried to control her response.

"Where will you be?" she asked tightly.

"I'll be spending the weekend at the beach. I have an appointment there on Friday so I thought I'd just stay in a boarding house and be ready to go on Monday morning."

"Oh. Well. That's great."

"Don't be angry. It would save me some time on the road, driving back here and then leaving again on Monday morning."

"Who said I was angry?"

"I can tell by the tone of your voice that you're not happy."

The pitch of Martha's voice went up. "I'm ecstatic. My husband is leaving me here so he can have fun at the beach."

"Martha, I'm not going to have fun. I'll be working all weekend."

"Uh huh."

"Well, don't try to make me feel guilty. I'm just trying my best to make enough money so we can have a good life."

"What type of life is this where you're gone all the time?"

"We have been over this again and again and I don't want to rehash it."

"Ok. Fine. I'll just see you whenever you decide to come home again."

Charles packed his bag and left that day. He didn't return until two weeks had passed. From then on he stayed away longer and Martha sometimes only saw him once a month. He did send money to her so she was able to stay in her house, but she wasn't able to afford much beyond minimum subsistence. She was resentful of his absences and let him know it when he did come home. Understandably, he found that his life was more pleasant when he was on the road than when he came home to her.

A solution came about when Martha applied her enterprising mind to the situation. Her brother Michael had a good job, and was paying rent on a small apartment. He was alone, having not yet gotten married, so he would be an easy housemate. He could help with living expenses at her house, rather than giving the money away to some landlord. She proposed the deal to Michael, who gladly moved into the spare bedroom. She didn't bother to mention the arrangement to Charles.

Two weekends after Michael had moved in, Charles came home. At first he seemed glad to see Michael since they were friends.

"Good to see you again Michael. What have you been up to?"

"Oh just working and moving," he answered.

"Oh, you moved? Where to?"

Silence.

"I moved in here with Martha." A puzzled look came over both the men's faces.

"Here? In our house?"

"Yes. Didn't Martha tell you?"

Martha started fidgeting in her seat. "I was going to tell you but I haven't seen you in a while so I just thought I'd tell you when you came home."

The silence was heavy.

Trying to cover his astonishment, Charles said slowly, "Well I guess that's okay. You can keep Martha company when I'm away."

"I just didn't realize that you didn't know I had moved in."

"This might work out well. You can help with some of the expenses."

"Yes, I guess that was the point."

Martha bustled into the kitchen and called out, "Is everyone ready to eat?"

And so the first night ended with all three people occupying the house in Alexandria. Charles was irritated with Martha going behind his back, but he realized that it was to his advantage that Michael was living there. It meant that Charles didn't have to feel guilty about leaving his wife on her own. He felt free to stay away for longer and longer times.

21

CHARLOTTE

Michael had been renting a room in his sister Martha's house for a few years before she acquired an additional boarder, Charlotte. Martha's husband Charles had long since moved out, presumably back to the Chicago area. As the courtship between Michael and his new friend Charlotte heated up, they discussed plans to marry. They agreed that they would not continue living with Martha. They wanted their own place, either in Alexandria or in neighboring Arlington. Michael would continue to help his sister financially, because her only income other than room rents was the money Charles still sent occasionally. But that didn't mean they couldn't move into their own place and have some privacy. Charlotte had a cordial, but not overly chummy, relationship with Martha.

Charlotte was a delicate woman, fair of complexion with curly blonde hair. One wouldn't call her beautiful, but she had a special grace about her that made her attractive. Not particularly outgoing, she was content to be a homemaker. She had moved in with Martha temporarily because her home situation with her parents was not good. Her father tended to drink too much and her mother was a meek woman, who wouldn't dare to cross her husband. Charlotte had a job taking care of children whose parents worked outside the home, which provided her with a small income. Martha, overbearing and bossy, saw she could take advantage of Charlotte's supposed weakness. Charlotte learned to stay out of the older woman's way to avoid conflict. She was prone to depression, and sudden severe headaches would send her to the bedroom, as often as once a week.

Martha was not very empathetic when these episodes occurred. She also held the somewhat inconsistent belief that Charlotte was too frail and delicate, and that if she would just eat more then she would feel better. She provided plenty of fattening foods for her boarders, but Charlotte didn't gain weight. And she kept having headaches.

One afternoon Michael came home early and found Charlotte in the fetal position in bed, moaning from the pain. He asked her if Martha had done anything to help ease the pain and Charlotte just whispered "No."

Confronting Martha, he asked if there wasn't anything that she could give Charlotte and she replied, "What can I do? She's sick and I'm not a nurse. She has a mental problem and probably needs to see a doctor."

"I'd think you could have tried to comfort her some way."

"Well I'm sorry she doesn't feel well but maybe you should do something."

Angered, Michael turned on his sister and raising his voice said, "Yes I think I should do something," and stalked out of the room.

That weekend Michael and Charlotte were married in Alexandria by a justice of the peace. They also started hunting for a house to move into so they could get away from Martha.

22

ON THEIR OWN

Michael and Charlotte had found a temporary home where some homeowners were renting rooms to young people. Charlotte and Michael's place was on the second floor, accessible by an outdoor stairway. The stairs were difficult for Charlotte to negotiate because she now was pregnant and the stairs were steep. She was careful, though, taking them slowly, as she didn't want anything to happen to her or to the unborn child. She felt fat and ungainly each time she climbed up or down. She had learned to cook and each night made a nutritious meal for herself and Michael. Now that she didn't have Martha watching her every move, she felt better. She still had occasional headaches, but their number and intensity had decreased.

She liked walking the streets of Alexandria, studying the architecture of the old buildings and imagining what life must have been like living there a hundred years before. The towering Masonic Temple was a comfort to her as it was visible from most places in the city. Union Station was also close by, and as Charlotte studied the brick building with the trains rumbling in and out, she wondered about the passengers riding the rails. Where were they going? Visiting family or friends in distant places? She was particularly intrigued with the cobblestone streets, many of which had been paved. Who carried all those stones and placed them just so to make it easier for carriages, horses and pedestrians to get around?

Returning home, Charlotte began preparations for Thanksgiving dinner. She had purchased a small turkey to cook since Michael had invited Martha to eat dinner with them. In a way Charlotte wasn't looking forward to entertaining Martha but since she was her sister in law, she felt it was her duty to be generous at this time of year. Tomorrow was Thanksgiving but she decided to make a couple of dishes ahead of time so she wouldn't be rushed on the big day. They expected Martha to come the next morning.

Charlotte was mixing the ingredients for her pumpkin pie when she began to feel queasy. She sat down until the feeling passed, hoping that the baby wasn't coming early. Soon after Michael came home from work. He took off his work clothes and came into the kitchen to help out with the preparations for the next day's big dinner. When he saw that Charlotte was looking pale, he became concerned.

"Are you feeling all right, honey?"

"I'm just a bit tired, but I'll feel better soon."

"Maybe you should go lie down. I'll work on dinner tonight."

"I might take you up on that," she replied.

And that night everything was fine.

The next morning Charlotte had an odd heavy sensation in her belly. The midwife had told her that she might feel something like that, but not to worry until she started having contractions. So Charlotte went on with dinner preparations. Just after noon, Martha knocked on the door and Michael let her in. Her gaze swept around the small and crowded living room, but she didn't make any comment. She settled herself into a wing chair in one corner and picked up a copy of the newspaper.

Michael asked, "Martha, Charlotte is in the kitchen making our dinner. Why don't you go in to say hello?"

She looked up at him as if he had suggested she make a trip to the moon, but then thought better of it and got up to go greet Charlotte. She paused in the doorway of the kitchen to regard her sister in law, who was swaying unsteadily and gripping the edge of the sink.

"Are you sick?"

"No, I'm just a bit fatigued. Oh, by the way, Happy Thanksgiving."

"Happy Thanksgiving to you too. You don't look well. Is the baby due?"

"Not for another few days but you never know."

"Well I don't know much about babies or births, but it seems to me that, as big as you are, it could happen any time now."

"I'll be fine. Why don't you go out to the living room and have Michael make you a drink?"

"I think I will," as she backed out of the room.

Michael was in the living room, fiddling with the leg of a table that was a bit wobbly.

"Michael, it looks like Charlotte could have the baby real soon."

All of a sudden they heard a little scream and Michael went running into the kitchen to find Charlotte on the floor clutching her stomach.

"Oh! It's time, isn't it, honey?"

"I think so. Could you see if you can get Mrs. Broadwell to come?" Mrs. Broadwell was a local midwife who delivered babies.

Michael was shaking but tried to keep calm. "I'll be back as soon as I can. Meanwhile Martha is here to stay with you."

Charlotte sighed and tried to get up. "Here, let me help you get into bed," Michael said.

He pulled her up gently and carried her into the tiny bedroom and settled her on the bed cover.

"Just hang on. You'll be fine," he tried to reassure her.

Martha was peering into the bedroom, looking a bit sick herself.

"Martha, I'm going to try to find the midwife. You stay here with Charlotte until I get back."

"But I don't know what to do. What if she has the baby while you're gone?"

"I think it takes a while before the baby is born and Charlotte will be having contractions. Just stay by her side until I return."

"Oh my. What about our dinner?" Martha asked, wringing her hands.

Michael ignored her and ran out the door.

"Martha, never mind about dinner," Charlotte wanly told her. "Just turn off the oven and all the pots. Michael can take care of it later." Looking like she wanted to flee, Martha stepped out and went in the kitchen to turn off the stove. She mumbled to herself, "Why oh why did this have to happen when I was here?"

She heard Charlotte gasp.

She poured herself a glass of wine and then thought that Charlotte might want one too so she carried two glasses into the bedroom.

"I brought you something to drink. Here, I'll leave it on the table."

Charlotte groaned and doubled up with pain. Martha thought she couldn't stand the noises that Charlotte was making so she figured she'd sing a few popular songs to drown out the pregnant woman's cries and possibly soothe Charlotte.

"When Irish Eyes are Smiling," she sang the tune loudly. She gulped some of her wine.

Charlotte just turned her head toward the wall.

"It's a Long, Long Way to Tipperary..." Martha crooned.

"Martha, please! Don't sing! I'm sick!"

"Oh, all right. I just thought it would cheer you up." Martha fidgeted in the chair and quickly sipped more wine. She finished her glass and started to drink the wine she had poured for Charlotte.

"Would you please get me a wet cloth for my forehead?" Charlotte asked Martha.

Martha stood up weaving a bit and grabbed the back of the chair for support. Singing more to herself than to Charlotte, "Over There, Over There" she found her way to the bathroom and brought the cloth to her sister in law.

Just then, Michael came in with Mrs. Broadwell. He saw Martha drinking wine, lounging on the bedside chair and humming the war song to herself and poor Charlotte in pain on the bed, clutching her stomach. It was all he could do to not explode but he knew his wife needed him at this critical time.

"Martha, since we won't be eating dinner tonight, why don't you go on home? I'll catch up with you later."

"Thank goodness! I thought you'd never get back," she said, stood up unsteadily, and wobbled out the front door.

23

ANDREW

Charlotte gave birth to a healthy baby boy. He had been born on Thanksgiving and his parents had given thanks for the delivery of a perfect baby. They named him Andrew, after his maternal grandfather. Charlotte adored her son and he became the center of her life. Michael was proud of him too, and together they would push the baby over Alexandria streets in his wicker pram. People would stop to admire the baby's full head of dark curly hair and his sweet expression. Sometimes they would visit Martha if she was home. Martha, not being a "baby person," didn't feel much affection toward Andrew. She never asked to hold the baby and didn't croon over him when she saw him. She would ask a perfunctory question about how he was doing, or make comments that he seemed to have grown, but she didn't seem very interested. She had little experience with babies, didn't much like babies, and had to force herself not to ignore him completely. One positive result of her antipathy towards infants was that she didn't show up to visit Charlotte and Michael nearly as often as she used to.

On Andrew's first birthday, his parents gave him a little party. They invited his Aunt Martha, their neighbor Edna, and Mrs. Broadwell, the midwife who had delivered him. Charlotte decorated the tiny dining area with blue balloons. She made him a cake with his name drawn in icing on top and a candle in the middle. There were some gifts wrapped gaily in blue wrapping paper piled up on the table. When the cake was cut, the guests admired the way Charlotte had dyed the white layers blue. Even Martha praised its light texture and scrumptious flavor.

Then it was time to open the presents. A small knitted cap with tiny matching booties from the midwife were displayed to be admired, next to a colorful rattle from the neighbor. Charlotte removed the paper from Martha's gift, and, as everyone looked to see what the box contained, there was silence. The guests stared at a full-size wooden baseball bat.

Martha said, "I thought the baby might like this when he gets a bit older. It's never too early to start playing baseball!"

Charlotte raised her eyebrows and tried to think of something appropriate to say.

Michael cleared his throat and said, "Thank you Martha. I'm sure Andrew will be able to use it in a few years."

Martha looked pleased with herself. Mrs. Broadwell rolled her eyes. Edna asked if she could have one more small piece of cake. The party went on and Andrew was none the wiser.

24

FREAK ACCIDENT

As the years went by, the little family settled into a routine. Michael worked during the day, while Charlotte stayed home with Andrew. The baby became a toddler and then a little boy. He was still too young to play with his baseball bat, but he had other age-appropriate toys to keep him busy. The baseball bat leaned against the back corner of the clothes closet, waiting for him to grow much taller. Charlotte was the model mother and housewife. Even though the family didn't have much money, she was able to put together nutritious meals every night. She enjoyed cooking and pleasing her husband. She blossomed under his attention. The crippling headaches were still a concern, but she was usually able to avoid them by avoiding stressful situations. They were too kind to say so out loud, but Michael and Charlotte both privately thought that the frequency of her headaches had become much more manageable since Martha rarely showed up at their door.

One day when the weather was warm, Charlotte decided to take Andrew for a walk in the sunshine. She dressed him in short pants and a sailor top with navy blue trim. Eager to go outside, he bounded down the outdoor steps and started running toward the street. Charlotte was just closing the door and turned around to see her little boy headed toward the busy street.

She cried out, "Andrew! Come back!"

He turned around to look at his mother and didn't see the car speeding along, close to him.

Charlotte screamed, "Andrew!!"

The car missed hitting him, but he fell down on the curb and started crying.

As Charlotte witnessed this scene playing out, she was thrown into a panic, and felt a terrific pain in her head. With the pain affecting her balance, and her haste to get to her son, she tripped over a stair tread and went tumbling down the steps, landing at the bottom. She was sprawled on the grass with her dress askew around her and was not moving. Andrew looked up and saw his mother lying there and wasn't sure of what to do.

He walked over to her and blinked. The tears were still fresh on his face as he said, "Mama. Mama. Get up, Mama."

Charlotte didn't move. Andrew just sat down in the grass beside her and patted her arm. "It's all right, Mama. Don't worry."

After a while, Edna, the neighbor, looked out her window and was horrified by what she saw. She ran outside and heard Andrew telling his mother that it was all right. Edna felt for a pulse and didn't find one. She turned Charlotte's head to one side and saw that she was lifeless. Edna thought she was going to be sick. Her mind went blank. Andrew patted her arm and said, "It's all right. Don't worry." He looked like he was in a trance. His eyes were glazed over and he kept staring at Charlotte's face. Charlotte wouldn't be able to see her precious son ever again.

25

PASSAGE OF TIME

Time passed at Lighthouse Point as it always had, slowly and without incident. The seasons changed, but Andrew no longer enjoyed the sunshine and fresh breezes or the sight of fall foliage. It felt as if he had been trapped alone in a frozen winter. He resumed his duties at the church, but they brought him little joy. His heart had grown heavy with the sadness of Taffy's passing. He didn't accept his fate to live the rest of his life without his beloved and decided that God had struck him down once again. Day by day he went about his business, doing his chores, preparing the Sunday sermons, but he didn't have the spark of life that he used to have before Taffy's death. His quick step had slowed and he seemed to trudge through each day as if he was carrying a weight on his shoulders.

His congregation still appreciated his presence, but they worried about him. They saw his newly downturned mouth, the wrinkles that seemed to have arrived overnight. Those who really looked at him were most hurt by the pain in his eyes. He looked ten years older. A few church members even started to speculate that he would never be himself again, and floated the idea of looking for a replacement. But the majority were loyal to him, and couldn't imagine adding that rejection to his burdens. Andrew was unaware of this talk, and possibly would not have cared if he did know. It seemed hard to care about anything anymore. His rods and reels were propped up in a corner of the utility room, sadly unused, gathering dust. His green boat, "Taffy" remained upside down near the dock as if he didn't have the strength or the heart to move it to his backyard. Whenever he walked by the boat, he didn't even glance at it. No one in the community commented on this and the boat slowly began to deteriorate on the shallow bank.

There were reminders of Taffy, and of the storm that took her, everywhere he looked. The house that Rosie saw blow away had not been rebuilt. The foundation stood cold and empty and was another sad reminder of the tragedy. Wisps of weeds grew up in the cracks of the cement and it looked forlorn and abandoned, which it was.

Some of the church ladies took Andrew under their wing. They invited him to their homes for dinner, or tried to tempt him with a picnic on a lovely day. When he and Taffy were together he had been gregarious, but now he rarely accepted invitations. The young women in their twenties and thirties might have taken an interest in him, but most had moved to bigger cities to find jobs or husbands. Even if they had approached him, Andrew would not have noticed.

He filled his days with church work. Periodically he would have a bout of depression, like he had when he was a teenager, living with Aunt Martha. His head would hurt and his eyes throbbed as he tried to go about his business, but many times he just had to retreat to the privacy of his bedroom and close the curtains and sleep. He believed that he would have to live with this debilitating state of mind for the rest of his life and that thought made him more depressed. Some days he was able to shake the sinking feeling and some days were bad. He felt so alone, even though he was surrounded with people from church and members of the community.

Early one bright morning, Samuel Gass approached Andrew's door. Samuel could see how broken his friend was, and consciously tried to balance his own actions. He didn't want to pester Andrew, who did need time to himself to get over his loss. He couldn't be expected to feel very sociable. On the other hand, Samuel didn't feel like it was healthy to have a man sitting by himself and brooding. So he showed up at the door once or twice a week, hoping that, one of those times, Andrew would be interested in having a little company.

Knocking on the door, Samuel called, "Andy, are you home?"

Andrew came to the door, still not dressed and looking disheveled.

"Yeah, come on in. Sorry I'm not very presentable."

"Is there anything I can get you? Anything I can do for you?"

"No, I'm fine. I just needed some extra sleep."

"How about if we take my boat out and see if there are any big ones to catch today?" Samuel asked.

"Oh no. I really don't want to go out on the water. I'll be ok; I just don't feel like doing much anymore."

"I'll be going into Leonardtown this weekend if you want to come along."

"I don't think so, Samuel. Besides, I have work to do at the church."

And so it went, month after month. The darkness threatened to envelop him, but he was hoping to find a way out of it. He knew that Taffy would not want him to give up on life. It was just that not much seemed to help.

Taffy's niece, Hialeah, drove up some weekends from Virginia to visit Andrew and usually attended the Sunday church service before leaving to go back home. He still marveled at her resemblance to Taffy. On Saturday nights they would play cards or just sit on the back porch enjoying the sunset, the sound of the night creatures on shore and in the water, and the rustling weeds. They were comfortable with each other, and her undemanding visits were the one bright point in his life now.

Rosie loved the summers, when her granddaughter Veronica stayed with her for weeks at a time. As she got older, the girl was becoming more of a help around the store. She knew how to stock the shelves, and she could sweep and tidy up. Her next goal was to be allowed to actually sell items, which involved making change from the cash register.

Veronica was Rosie's only grandchild, but she might have been the favorite even if that weren't the case. Their personalities were similar, and some of the townspeople even referred to Veronica as "Rosie Junior." Veronica did have more love for animals than Rosie did, although that could have been because she was still young enough to not fully appreciate how much work it was to have a pet. She told anyone who asked that she was going to be a veterinarian when she grew up.

The summer days and nights when the kids danced to those great old songs on the transistor radio and the cat family took up residence on the dock were peaceful and serene. No major weather events disturbed the hamlet. The car crash was one unfortunate happening. The little black kitten gradually regained his mobility, even though he would limp for the rest of his life. Veronica, along with the mother cat, nursed him back to health over a period of weeks. All three cats started to get used to a diet of Puss n Boots canned cat food. Instead of spending their nights prowling around the dock, they stayed close to the store's front porch.

One day, Veronica, at Rosie's urging, set up a box on the porch with a hand drawn sign on cardboard that read, "Free Kitens." Not distracted by the misspelling, people stopped by to pet them and remark on how cute they were. At the end of the day Teddy had come by and said his Aunt Evonne in Lusby, Maryland wanted the black and white mama tuxedo. The two kittens remained. Veronica finally persuaded her mother to allow her to adopt the mischievous black one. She promptly named him "Havoc", such an appropriate name for the little one.

The gray and white kitten remained, unclaimed. Before it got dark, Rosie came out on the porch and saw the little feline playing with a leaf on the porch.

"You're still here? I would have thought someone would take you home!" She went back inside the store and came out with a small dish of cat food, which the kitten devoured.

"Maybe tomorrow you'll find a home. Let's put you back in the box for tonight," as she picked up the furry one and placed her in the cardboard box.

The next day, the kitten was up early, trying to scratch her way out of the high-sided box. She flexed her sharp little claws but couldn't quite reach the top of the box. So she patiently waited for someone to lift her out. A gray-haired lady from down the street was up and about early and as she climbed the steps to the store, looked down at the writing on the box's front.

"Well, hello!" she exclaimed as she saw the pretty kitten watching her. "You're free, huh? I'd take you home but Benny probably wouldn't like it. He likes being an only dog." With a smile, she continued into the store to pick up some coffee. Even though she wasn't able to take the kitten home, she felt cheered by the sight of the pretty little creature.

All day long people came and went, doing their grocery shopping. Some smiled at the kitten, some picked her up and stroked her. No one heard her meow. Rosie continued to feed her and put out a dish of water for her to drink. She started wondering whether anyone was going to adopt the kitten and if she was going to have to take care of the little cat forever. A couple more days passed with no takers. Rosie was beginning to despair. She liked cats but didn't need the responsibility of a pet.

Later that week, Andrew stopped by the store to pick up some groceries. The gray and white kitten was all alone playing with a small toy in the box. Her brother and mother had already gone to their new homes days before. As soon as the kitten heard Andrew's footsteps on the stairs, she peeked out of the top of the box at him and extended her paw towards him. He bent down to rub her head and she lifted her chin up to be scratched.

"Well, are you the only one left? Your mother and brother have found homes and you haven't?" he asked her. She opened her mouth as if to respond but no meow was forthcoming. It was a silent meow.

"You don't really have a voice, do you?"

No response, just a sweet look on her face as she watched him go into the store. Rosie was behind the counter, and saw the exchange between the man and the kitten.

"Andrew, why don't you take the kitten home with you? She seems to like you and she really needs a home. Besides, she would be good company for you."

"What would I do with a cat? I've never even had a cat."

"I just think she needs you and you might even need her."

Andrew chuckled. "I think you would just like to not have to worry about her anymore."

Rosie replied, "She's no trouble, not like her brother was. Veronica took him home a few days ago."

"Well, I don't know. I'll think about it," he said, not really meaning it as he was leaving the store.

The kitten was waiting for him as if she knew what her destiny was, extended her arms, stood up on her hind legs, grasped the side of the box and hoisted herself out and started following Andrew home. At first he didn't notice her but then she ran around in front of him and stopped, wiggled her rear end and playfully pounced on his shoe.

"It looks like you want to go home with me, but I don't need a kitten. Why don't you just go back to the store so someone who really likes cats can take you?"

She reached up to rub around his leg. He tried to ignore her, but she kept getting in his way and he had to walk around her to avoid tripping.

"Ok, come on. Let's see what I have for dinner. I'll feed you but then you have to go back."

It was comical to see the mini parade of the minister and the little feline following him all the way to his house. The kitten had a purposeful step and a waving tail as she boldly followed her new friend. As they arrived at Andrew's house, he unlocked the door and the kitten scampered inside. He stood there looking a bit perplexed since he really didn't want her inside the house. He wasn't prepared to have a cat indoors.

Andrew found a small saucer and poured some milk in it and set it on the kitchen floor. The little furball lapped it up and then licked her paws and washed her face. As Andrew went about fixing himself some dinner, the kitten disappeared somewhere in the house. He wasn't too concerned at first but after dinner he started to search for her and found her fast asleep in the middle of his bed. Not wanting to disturb her, he let her sleep and tiptoed out to the back porch to write in his diary. He thought to himself that things were turning upside down and he would have this furry kitten moving in with him and he wasn't sure he liked it.

Dear Diary,

Today a kitten followed me home. She was the last kitten left from the cat family that hangs out on the dock. She had followed me home one time before, but I hadn't seen much of her lately. What will I do with her? I don't know much about cats. She seems to have something wrong, because she never meows. She opens her mouth but she doesn't say anything. Now I need to think of a suitable name. She's gray and white, so maybe "Whitey?" No, too common. She has a lot of personality, so maybe "Perky?" No, I don't like that. "Sweetie?" "Precious?" "Fuzzy?" No, not quite the right name. I'll think about it.

My thoughts still turn to my beloved Taffeta every day, especially when I walk past the church. Occasionally I put wildflowers on her grave, even knowing that she isn't in there. But I'm comforted by the thought that she is in heaven with Jesus, waiting for me to join her.

This coming weekend Hialeah will be visiting. I always look forward to seeing her. I know one day she'll probably get married and have children and then she won't be coming to visit so often, but I'll enjoy it while I can.

Maybe we can have blue crabs for dinner, if there are any in the trap. I hope the headaches won't keep me down while she's here.

Well I'd better get back to see what this kitten is doing.

He found her still asleep on his bed and decided to take a nap with his new housemate, even if it was just a temporary situation. The kitten cuddled up to him as they both snoozed in the gathering dusk.

26

SILENT MEOW

Early the next morning he was awakened by a feather tickling his face. He tried to brush it away but it kept coming back. Groggily he opened his eyes and saw two somber green eyes peering at him from the other pillow. Confused, he sat upright and then remembered.

"Oh my. What have I done?" A soft paw touched his hand. Andrew thought she must be hungry, so he left his cozy bed to find her something to eat.

Hialeah arrived late that afternoon, exhausted from having made her way through the Washington DC traffic. She knocked on Andrew's door and as he opened it, the kitten came bounding out to greet her.

"Well! Who are you? Aren't you adorable?" she exclaimed. "Andrew, I didn't know you had a kitten."

"I've only had her since yesterday. She sort of followed me home. She adopted me but I really don't want to keep her."

Hialeah bent down to pick her up and the kitten nuzzled her neck.

"I'm enchanted! She's just what you needed! A little furry friend to keep you company."

"My intention was to keep her outside but she just moved right in yesterday. I'm going to set up a box on the back porch for her to sleep in."

"Does she have a name yet?"

"No, I've been watching her and trying to come up with a suitable name but nothing has really been the right one yet. Come on in and I'll fix you a drink and we can sit on the porch before dinner."

Dinner consisted of a pile of blue crabs, steaming fresh from the pot and seasoned just right. Andrew spread a layer of newspapers on the table and found his nutcrackers and picks to remove the small bits of crab from their shells. A person who hasn't eaten fresh crabs in the shell might think that the slow process of extracting the bits of meat was a problem. In fact, the leisurely pace just added to their enjoyment. A green salad and some iced tea completed the meal. Hialeah had picked up some ice cream at Rosie's, and that, with a few cookies, was dessert.

Later, after everything had been cleaned up, they were relaxing in the rocking chairs and watching the night sky for falling stars. The kitten joined them and jumped up into Andrew's lap and settled in.

"It's funny how she never meows. She opens her mouth as if she would, but I've never heard her say anything," Andrew told Hialeah. "I wonder why she does this? Maybe it's because she's special and different from other cats."

Hialeah looked at the kitten and exclaimed, "Taffy! She wasn't able to speak and neither can the kitten! What do you think of naming her after Aunt Taffeta?"

Andrew sat there for a moment, stroking the kitten.

"Well I suppose Taffy might be honored to have this little one named after her."

"Then, Taffy it is."

As if the kitten knew the conversation was about her, she reached up and put her paw on Andrew's arm.

"Taffy. Taffy. We will call you Taffy after my lovely wife."

Taffy just kneaded Andrew's arm in contentment as Hialeah smiled at both of them. Andrew was feeling relaxed and calm, without the cloud of depression that had hung over him for so long. He was suddenly struck by inspiration.

"Do you think you want to try your luck fishing tomorrow? We can fish off the dock and I think it's supposed to be a nice day," Andrew asked Hialeah.

"Ok, but I guess that means I need to get up early."

"I'll let you sleep until 7:00."

"Oh well, thanks a lot. I really don't mind getting up early when I'm here. I've come to appreciate the slow pace of Lighthouse Point. It's so much different from the hustle and bustle of Washington. I think in years to come I might like to retire here," she responded.

"I love it here. But you'd have to get used to not being able to go shopping in department stores unless you drive back to the District. Of course there is a store in Leonardtown that sells ladies' clothes. And there's a good grocery store there too. Oh, and there's a wonderful Methodist church right down the street here."

"But how about the minister? Is he a good preacher?" she teased.

"I've heard some people say he's ok."

The next morning, they ate an early breakfast before gathering the fishing gear. As they headed down the road toward the dock, they were trailed by the newly-named Taffy. Sassy tail held high, she would stop every now and then to examine things of interest to a cat. Bugs crossing the road and movements in the weeds had to be investigated before she could continue on her way. Coming up to the dock, she scurried ahead since she was so familiar with this place. She went right to the dock's end and lay down so she could check out the crab trap. It was empty but the sloshing water was interesting enough to rate some attention.

"Those crabs were delicious last night, Andrew," Hialeah said.

"Some people think it's too much trouble to crack the shells and extract what little meat is there, but I think that's half the fun."

Hialeah looked pensive and asked, "Do you think you'll move the boat any time?"

Andrew hesitated before answering. "I don't know. I guess in a way it reminds me of the last time Taffy was in it. She took it out trying to catch us some fish for dinner and then it turned tragic. Her last act was for my benefit."

"She loved you so much, Andrew. The letters she sent to me were always full of news about you, your work at the church and things you did together."

"I think about her every day. She still lives in my heart and always will."

They were silent for a while. Taffy the kitten turned over on her back and playfully reached out to Andrew. He rubbed her tummy and smiled at her.

They fished for a while. Neither minded that their catch consisted entirely of small ones that had to be thrown back.

"Let's go see if Rosie has made any ham sandwiches. I'd like one for lunch," Andrew said. "I'll buy you a Coca Cola too."

They packed up their gear and walked down the shell path to the store, followed by Taffy.

As they passed the church, they saw Samuel Gass pulling weeds in the rose garden.

"Hi!"

"When you're through here, you can always come down to my house to pull some weeds," Andrew told him.

"Reverend, my work at the church is never done but if it is I'll help you out. Here, let me cut you some Peace roses to put on Taffeta's grave."

"How lovely! And they smell heavenly," Hialeah exclaimed.

"What would you expect? They're growing in the church yard."

Little Taffy ambled up to greet Samuel.

"I see you have a new companion, Andrew."

"Yep. Hialeah named her Taffy."

"Taffy!"

"Neither one has ever spoken so we thought it was a good name for her."

"Well, she's a cute little thing."

"Thanks for the roses, Samuel."

They walked over to Taffeta's headstone and placed the roses on the ground. Little Taffy disappeared in the cemetery and after a while they saw her dragging something in her mouth towards them.

"What's this?" Hialeah asked.

"Oh it's just Stan Teeter's teeth."

Hialeah looked puzzled and then amused as Andrew told her the story of the dentures.

They replaced the teeth on Stan's gravestone and went on their way home.

The next day Hialeah took out her dress to wear to church. Andrew had already gone ahead to prepare for the morning's service. She was running a little late so she pulled her shoes on and grabbed her purse and started down the road toward the church. Taffy followed behind her and about halfway there, Hialeah looked back and saw the kitten.

"Taffy! Go on back home!"

Taffy sat down in the road and looked at Hialeah as she continued on her way. Then, sprinting to catch up, Taffy pursued the young woman hurrying to get to church on time.

"Taffy! You need to go home! They won't let a cat in the church!"

Ignoring Hialeah as only a cat can do, Taffy ran heedlessly ahead and disappeared at the top of the church steps.

"Yes we'll gather at the river. The beautiful, the beautiful river," sang the choir.

Hialeah slipped in the door and found a seat in the back, hopefully unnoticed by the church members. Andrew saw her and winked at her. At that moment, Taffy appeared from behind the door. Spying Andrew at the front, she prissed her way slowly down the aisle, directly toward him. Several people chuckled. As more eyes turned toward the small feline making tracks toward her intended, Andrew watched her, speechless.

"*Soon our happy hearts will quiver, with the melody of peace.*"

Andrew nodded at the choir and said, "Peace be with you. Good morning, everyone."

The congregation replied, "Good morning."

Taffy settled herself next to Andrew.

"I see we have a visitor this morning," he said. "This is my new kitten, Taffy." He heard a few gasps from the people in the pews.

"We named her 'Taffy' because she has no voice, just like my own beloved Taffy. She chose to live with me and I know you might be offended that she's here in church. If you object, I'll put her back in my office for the next hour."

"No, let her stay!" came a voice from the front pew.

"She's not hurting anyone and she might need to soak up a little religion," someone else chimed in. Scattered chuckles and murmurs of assent were audible from the back. Andrew scanned the congregation and didn't see anyone who seemed concerned.

And so, the Sunday service continued while Taffy tucked her paws underneath herself and watched the proceedings.

27

HOMES FOR THE KITTENS

Veronica's black kitten, Havoc, was content in his new home with Veronica and her mother, Irene. They lived in a comfortable house, set back from the highway. Even though he still seemed to look for trouble, Veronica paid a lot of attention to him. That, and memories of his close call with the car, helped keep him out of trouble. There was no water near their home to tempt him, so he stayed around the house, chasing bugs and enjoying this new life of soft beds and pampering. His body had filled out now that he was eating regularly. His coat almost sparkled like black diamonds in the sunlight and his emerald green eyes were busy watching life happen. He bonded with Veronica, and loved her best of all, but was content seeking attention from Irene when the girl went to visit Rosie. He limped slightly but it didn't slow him down.

Teddy's Aunt Evonne, who had adopted Havoc's mother, named the cat Amiga because she was so friendly. Amiga didn't seem to miss her kittens after the first few days of moving to Lusby with Evonne. After acquainting herself with new surroundings and adjusting to being an indoor/outdoor cat, she turned her attention to her new humans, Evonne and Fred. They had been thinking about adopting a cat and Amiga seemed to be the perfect fit. Amiga settled into a life of snoozing on a comfortable chair, receiving a lot of attention from her human housemates and playing with her new bunny rabbit friends, Jazz and Tango. The bunnies had lived with cats before, and soon the threesome could sometimes be seen napping together in the sun. Evonne was relieved that they got along so well. She had been wanting another cat ever since their elderly Licorice died, but had been hesitant about bringing one into the house with the rabbits. Now she had a new cat who resembled her beloved former pet, and who fit in so well. Amiga seemed relieved that she no longer needed to hunt to provide food for herself and two kittens. Food magically appeared twice a day, and her human housemates provided companionship whenever she tired of the bunnies.

All three cats were lucky to have been adopted into loving homes. Being meow-less didn't seem to be a problem for Taffy. Andrew hadn't owned a cat before, but it seemed to him that a meow is important communication. He thought that cats meow to attract attention, to ask for food, to have the door opened, or to demand that their human figure out what it is they want and give it to them. They most often meow at people but will sometimes meow at other cats. His wife Taffy had communicated by writing and gestures, but (Andrew thought, to his own amusement) even if this little Taffy could write, her note would always just say 'Meow.' He had to pay attention to her expressive face, ears and tail. She might have a desperate look on her face while she was standing close to the door, looking back and then at the door. Andrew knew she wanted to go out to relieve herself. And sometimes she just wanted to go out and then run right back inside. She would also jump on the table when he was working and position herself on his papers and give him a wide-eyed look, essentially saying, "Pay attention to me!" He was fascinated by her silent communication. The bond between the kitten and the man grew. Slowly Taffy trained Andrew to do what she wanted.

Taffy settled into Andrew's life quickly, as if she had been waiting for him to rescue her. Despite his half-hearted efforts to coax her to sleep in the box on the porch, she steadfastly insisted on sleeping on his bed. She curled up next to his legs so closely that, if he wanted to get out of bed, he had to slide out like a mummy so as not to disturb her. Growing into an attractive and dainty young cat, she tagged along after Andrew whenever he walked around the neighborhood. His friends smiled when they saw them together and were glad that he had a companion to keep his mind off the pain of losing Taffeta. She never had the inclination to stay on the dock or wander away to explore when she saw him heading towards their home. All in all, she was a delightful kitten.

Her second favorite place had become the Methodist church on Sundays or any time that Andrew was working in his office. At times she would settle herself on the family Bible that had belonged to Taffeta's family and watch Andrew as he pecked at the old typewriter. The clacking of the keys was especially fascinating to her. She also became a fixture on Sunday mornings, stationing herself at the front door to greet the church members as they entered. Most of them had come to expect her presence each week and looked forward to seeing her.

The summer's heat faded into the relief of fall. The kids who hung out in back of the church now studied their lessons in the evenings and went to the football games on Friday nights. Sometimes on Saturday nights a few would congregate on the basketball court behind the church, smoking cigarettes and sometimes drinking beer, which they hid in soft drink bottles. As the weather cooled, fewer and fewer of them stayed outside, preferring someone's basement when the parents weren't home. Stan Teeter's teeth remained on his headstone.

When school started again in the fall, Veronica started a new year at school and wasn't able to spend as much time with Havoc. She loved him dearly, and didn't want him to feel bored or neglected, so she made a point of spending time with him when she first got home each afternoon. She was outgrowing the stage where playing with her Barbie doll had been her favorite activity. She now spent her allowance on teen magazines, which she read on the front porch swing while Havoc napped in her lap. She loved stroking his soft fur, so thick and healthy now that he had a regular diet.

"Havoc! What have you been into today?" She asked her kitten. There was a small pile of toilet tissue on the bathroom floor that had been scratched off the roll. Havoc had an innocent look on his face.

"This is a big mess! Now I have to clean it up." Veronica bent down to pick up the tissue and Havoc jumped into the middle of the pile.

"You are so silly!" She dangled a bit of tissue over his head and he grabbed it with his paws. He snatched it up in his mouth and carried it out the door into the living room.

She went running after him, laughing. They entertained each other every day.

Hialeah continued to visit Andrew and Taffy the kitten. She had inherited some money from her grandmother a few years previously and decided to buy a small cottage at Lighthouse Point, which was a fixer-upper. Spending time there on the weekends, wallpapering or painting a room, gave her great pleasure.

She loved to see the results of her handiwork as the little house improved and would one day become habitable. Barely larger than her apartment in Northern Virginia, it consisted of a small living room, one bedroom that accommodated a single bed, a tiny kitchen and a few square feet of bathroom with a stand-up shower. The artesian well produced a lot of good water but she would have to get the house rewired when she saved up more money. Her plans were to use the cottage as a getaway from the intensity of the Washington area. The cottage provided no view of the water, but it was just a short distance away and she could hear it whispering when she had the windows open at night. Andrew was just down the road, and she had begun to get acquainted with some of the townspeople. And of course, Rosie was always available for a chat or for help getting supplies for the renovation.

Andrew's diary entry one day that fall:

> *Dear diary,*
>
> *I'm thankful for so many things in my life that I don't know where to begin. Thank the Good Lord for the changing of the seasons when we get a reprieve from the relentless heat of summer. I am so blessed to live in such a quiet and peaceful place as Lighthouse Point where I have a job that I love and friends who care about me. I treasure the friendship of Hialeah as my only remaining family*

member. I pray that God will watch over her as she fixes up her little house here. And finally I have come to love my kitten, Taffy. She is a great comfort to me every day and I know she was sent to me for this reason. Sometimes I can almost feel the presence of Taffeta, my beloved, as I look into the sweet face of my kitten. This may sound silly but I think Taffeta is with me in many ways. The whisper of the leaves as they fall to the ground, the stars that pinpoint the night sky and the softness of little Taffy's fur when I pet her all make me envision Taffeta by my side. These are things she would have loved too. I haven't had a headache for a few weeks and I'm grateful for that.

28

THE LOVE OF A CAT

The crippling headaches didn't affect Andrew as much as they had for the past few years. He would never reconcile himself to the fact that his Taffeta would never be with him as long as he lived, but he accepted the grief reluctantly. The talk amongst the church members about finding a new minister had ceased and Andrew never knew that some people had wanted to replace him. He quietly went about his church work to calm him and temporarily forget about his troubles.

His cat Taffy had grown into a petite and beautiful feline. She still followed Andrew whenever he left the yard and his neighbors teased him about her being his shadow. She was a fixture at the church every Sunday morning. Several members remarked that she had soaked up so much religion that she would occupy a special place in heaven once she left this earth. Andrew simply adored her. He bought her the best cat food and let her do whatever she wanted. If she jumped up on the kitchen counter, he would talk to her as she watched him prepare his meals. The cardboard box that he originally intended for her to sleep in was now used for storing old books. The cat was a comforting fixture on his bed every night.

Andrew would sit on his back porch and watch her as she went about her cat business. He began to think that she was sent to him for a purpose, and he may have been right, in that she knew when he didn't feel well. If a headache was keeping Andrew down, Taffy stayed by his side, purring, and the sound and vibrations from her throat seemed to help relieve the intense pain. She would even wrap herself around his head on the pillow to help banish the headache. The cat seemed to sense that her presence relieved his suffering. Even though he had never owned a cat, Andrew thought she was perfect and believed that there was no better furry companion anywhere. As she gazed at Andrew, Taffy would blink her eyes slowly, communicating her trust and love for her human friend. Andrew would smile and pat the seat next to him signaling his desire for her to sit on his lap, which she usually did. Curling up together, they would nap for a while, easing the stress he felt when his thoughts turned back in time to that terrible night and the days following the tropical storm. He believed that if he could live through that tragedy he could possibly face any other obstacle that came his way. He was horribly wrong.

29

MID-1960s

The Beatles created a hysteria among young women that hadn't been witnessed since the days of the young Frank Sinatra or that of Elvis Presley. More than that, the British Invasion had changed popular music. It enraged some parents, entranced the boys as well as the girls, and had an impact on fashion. Boys grew their hair to resemble the English mop tops and girls sported long straight hair to go with mini skirts and fishnet hose. Everything mod came from England. Folk music and some early protest songs were on the charts. Young people were rebelling against their parents, "The Establishment", schools and wherever else they could find a cause.

In Lighthouse Point the styles were adopted a bit slower than in larger cities, but the music was the center point around which many other things revolved.

It was an unsettling time for much of the nation and Lighthouse Point was no exception.

Veronica and Teddy had changed too. Both young teenagers, they were still friends and had decided to remain friends instead of exploring a different kind of relationship.

Havoc slept on Veronica's bed each night and played in the yard. Fortunately, given his history, the house was well back from the street where any traffic that went by was slow. Perhaps it was because he had so much space of his own, or possibly he had some memory of what had happened on the road in front of Rosie's store, but Havoc never ventured near the street at his new home.

The local kids still hung out at the back of the Methodist church on Friday and Saturday nights unless there was a football game to attend. Some of the older boys and a few girls still smoked cigarettes in the dark, trying to act sophisticated. The unusually warm weather had persisted into late fall which brought out the teenagers who would usually be indoors at this time of year. Someone would bring their portable record player and hook it up to an outside electrical outlet. This allowed them to bring their own 45s from home and play favorite songs over and over just by moving the machine's arm.

One Friday night, the teens were out later than usual, enjoying the balmy weather. A group of boys were standing around talking about the Washington

Redskins and the streak of losses they had been experiencing. Some girls were laughing and whispering, talking about the boys on the other side of the basketball court. Someone had brought a record, "My Girl" by the Temptations and was playing it over and over. Some of the girls glanced over at the boys, wishing they would ask them to dance, but football scores took priority over slow dancing. Veronica and Teddy were sitting on a bench, talking about nothing in particular. The girl had blossomed into a striking young lady who sometimes drew glances from the older boys. She mostly ignored them. She was as tall as Teddy and the summer sun had bleached her hair to a golden blonde color. After a while she said to Teddy, "I think I'll go on in now. Do you want to go fishing tomorrow?"

"Yeah, ok. Do you want to meet at the dock at 7:00?"

"Sounds good. I'll bring some crickets. Maybe there'll be some crabs in the cage by then too."

"Ok. Goodnight."

"See you then."

Veronica flipped her hair over her shoulder and walked through the side yard toward the store. She heard a boy whistle at her but she didn't turn around. She wasn't a dog that could be called by a whistle. At this point in her life, her interests didn't include boys. When she reached the store, she quietly let herself in since she knew Rosie would probably be sleeping. The last thing she did was set her alarm clock for 6:30 a.m.

Andrew was at his table on the back porch, working on his Sunday sermon. Taffy was reclining on the back of his chair, occasionally swiping her tail across his face. He would laugh and reach around to pet her. She never tried to claw him; she would sometimes tap him with claws sheathed to get his attention. Over the past few years, their relationship had blossomed into love. The cat loved the man and that feeling was reciprocated. Andrew wondered how he had ever lived without his little Taffy. He truly believed that there were no other perfect cats in the world. She had no bad habits and didn't scratch the furniture inside. She did have a favorite oak tree outside that bore the marks of her handiwork. She was as devoted to him as any feline could be. Andrew thought they must have been predestined to be together as she had eased him out of his depression and he had saved her when no one else wanted her. His debilitating headaches had disappeared soon after she had moved in a couple of years before.

Taffy jumped onto the table and started to chew on the end of Andrew's pencil. He played with her for a while and then said, "I think it's time for us to turn in. I'll finish the last part of the sermon tomorrow." Taffy followed him into the bedroom and after he was settled, she jumped up and wrapped herself around his head and began to knead his hair and scalp. He reached up to scratch her underneath her chin and she lifted her head up to enjoy it. Both fell asleep shortly.

Meanwhile in the back of the church, the girls had gone home but a few boys remained. They no longer played the records but a couple had moved off into the darker part of the woods to smoke some Marlboros. The dry fall leaves crackled underfoot as the boys inhaled and exhaled the toxic fumes. They flicked the ashes onto the ground. A few leaves caught fire and the boys laughed and stomped out the small sparks. It was time to go home, so they did their best to make sure that nothing else was burning. Smelling like the bottom of an ashtray, they headed home, where each would swear to his parents that he had not been smoking.

Unseen to the boys, a small eruption had occurred under a pile of leaves. It was kindled by the dryness and availability of many leaves that had fallen. The edges of leaves caught and crinkled, putting forth a stream of smoke that smelled like a cozy fireplace in the winter. Spreading slowly at first, it soon picked up speed and had moved from its original small circle to a larger one, heading toward the back of the church. The line of fire followed the pathway, igniting small underbrush. The sound intensified as the fire moved faster. The darkened church beckoned and the old wooden walls presented themselves as perfect tinder. No one was around to see the destruction that had already made itself apparent and no one would become aware of its force for hours.

Andrew and Taffy slept soundly together. She had moved to curl herself in the crook of his legs and prop her head up on this soft pillow. Several hours had passed when the cat woke up for some reason.

The fire spit and popped as it snaked its way down the path to where the kids had played basketball, where they had danced to the old 60s songs and where they had kissed their sweethearts. The flames incinerated anything in the way as it methodically moved toward its target. Gathering strength, it caught one of the wooden benches and slowly began to consume the legs. Fueled by the dry wood, it now added the dimension of height, as flames flickered in the air.

The smell of burning leaves carried by the smoke started to drift out of the woods. An acrid stew of burnt leaves mixed with charred wood arose to choke out the crisp autumn air. The fire moved closer to the church.

Taffy instinctively knew something was wrong. As she awakened fully, her highly-tuned senses were on the alert. She smelled the smoke, in spite of the distance of her house from the church. Her whiskers twitched and she jumped out of bed. Padding through the house, she made her way to the partially-opened porch door, which was left cracked so she could go in and out at night. Pausing on the back porch, she sniffed the danger. Her hackles began to rise and her striped tail fluffed out.

She started running in the direction of the church, down the road she had trod so often, on her way to church or following Andrew as he ran errands around Lighthouse Point. As she approached the building, she could see the flames in the back yard, which had by now reached the structure. This was where Andrew's small office was and Taffy had spent many a lazy afternoon with him napping on the small desk while he worked.

She stood still, taking in the scene, tail bristling. The fire scared her and she backed away toward the parking area. No one was in sight; most people had already gone to bed. The clear night sky now had a filmy haze over it, blocking out the stars. She opened her mouth to meow but she made no sound.

Now, on a mission, she ran back down the road to her home. Panting a bit from her run, she squeezed through the porch door and sprang up on the bed, where Andrew was quietly sleeping. She walked hurriedly around the bed top and nosed her way under the covers. Andrew didn't stir. She popped out and walked across his chest and flicked her tail in his face. He groggily brushed away the tail. Still trying to wake him, the cat tried to cry out but the effort was useless. She looked down at his face and breathed on his eyes. No response. Finally, she knew she had to resort to an act that she had never had to employ before. Taffy reached out and scratched Andrew's cheek.

"Ow! What the...? What are you doing?" a surprised Andrew asked her. He touched his cheek and could feel a trickle of blood. He was confused and a bit angry. The cat was agitated and swung her body around and around as she looked wildly at him. Andrew's forehead wrinkled into a frown.

"What is it? Why did you scratch me?" Taffy had never lifted a claw to him before. She jumped down and jumped back up repeatedly. Andrew by now was wide awake and becoming alarmed. He thought little Taffy might be sick or had gone crazy. He swung his legs out of bed as he watched his cherished kitty opening and closing her mouth while watching him. She ran to the back of the house and looked over her shoulder to see if Andrew was following. He pulled on some pants and a shirt and followed her outside. She started to run down the driveway and it was then that Andrew smelled the sickening odor of the smoke. He knew it was not someone's fireplace. He ran after his cat toward the church and saw a horrible sight. The church, his church, was in flames. The orange and yellow blaze was rapidly consuming the structure.

He started hyperventilating as he tried to keep up with Taffy. He felt nauseated from the combination of unusual physical exertion and horror. The glow from the fire and the intensity of the heat was almost overwhelming. He stopped in the parking area, staring, as his mind tried to process the awful sight of the inferno in front of him. Andrew's legs wouldn't take him any further. He sank down to the ground and then he felt a soft touch on his arm. Taffy was circling him, marking him with her whisker pads, claiming him as her own. Gradually his mind began to work again and he realized there was something he had to do.

30

BURNING!

Veronica awoke to the sound of someone shouting. She sat up and peered out the window of her room above the store. Shocked, she saw the Methodist church burning and someone kneeling in the oyster shell parking area in front. She ran to Rosie's room and knocked loudly and shouted, "Grandma! Wake up! The church is on fire!"

Rosie was groggy from her sound sleep, but as soon as she heard the word, "fire" she woke up in a hurry.

"Veronica! Go ring the bell!"

Veronica ran down the steps and flew out the door. She pulled the heavy chain and the bell tolled its mournful sound, just as it had in that tragic year when Taffeta drowned.

Bong! Bong! Bong! Such an ominous sound.

She kept ringing it until her arms were tired. She looked up and saw a cloud of smoke rising through the treetops. The burning smell was almost too much so she went back inside the store where Rosie was now on the phone trying to call someone at the volunteer fire department.

Meanwhile, in back of the church, the smoke was as thick as a morning fog on the coast of Maine. Andrew could barely see his own hand in front of his face. He quickly made his way to the office, or what remained of it. He knew he had to get the old family Bible that had belonged to Taffeta. He hoped that it hadn't burned in the fire. His faithful cat, Taffy, trailed him around the side yard and followed him to the back. Andrew unbuttoned his shirt and wrapped it around his nose and mouth to ward off the smoke. The heat emanating from the church was blistering but Andrew was going in to try to rescue the Bible. It was as important to him as it had been to Taffeta. The history of her family had been written by hand on the back pages and he knew the Bible itself dated back at least a hundred years and maybe more. He had used it on most Sundays during church services in his tenure at the church.

He knew exactly where he had left it, which was on the right hand side of his small desk. Suddenly a passage from the book of Isaiah came to his mind "... when you walk through fire you shall not be burned, and the flame shall not consume you." Andrew took this as a message that he was to go ahead with his plan of saving Taffeta's Bible.

Stepping through the remains of the back door, he glanced backward and saw little Taffy trying to follow him. He shouted, "No! Go back Taffy!" Unused to him shouting, she paused, watching her human companion step through the doorway. Again she moved toward him and the intense heat singed her whiskers. Unsure of his motives, she kept her eyes on him and twitched her tail.

31

FIRE

Everyone within a mile of the store woke up when they heard the bell, their dreaded signal that there was a tragedy unfolding. Men who had quickly pulled on jeans and flannel shirts appeared outside in the dark, and immediately sensed or saw what was happening. About six of them, including Samuel Gass, ran toward the store and burst inside. Rosie was on the phone, trying to explain the situation to a half-asleep member of the nearest volunteer fire department. Veronica wanted to help but couldn't think of a single thing that she could do. The men excitedly discussed how they could get water from the river to try to put out the flames and decided on the bucket method. This entailed running back home to grab whatever buckets they had and then forming a line, carrying the water from the river as fast as they could to throw on the fire. Several more men joined in, helping to shorten the time the buckets were filled. No one ever thought that anyone would actually be in the church, given the time of night. After a few feeble attempts to curtail the spread of the fire, the men became more adept at keeping the water coming and concentrated their efforts at the front of the church, which had not yet begun to burn.

Rosie issued her granddaughter a stern warning to stay away from the church and not go near the mens' fire line. Veronica did take care to keep out of the way, but she had to see what was happening. She carefully skirted the area and, coming up on the back side of the church, saw something she would never forget. She blinked her eyes a couple of times trying to adjust them to the darkness and the scene in front of her.

32

THE BIBLE

If Andrew had been thinking calmly, he might have questioned his irresistible impulse to save Taffeta's Bible. But there was no thinking clearly in the midst of a conflagration. His beloved cat had stared at him with wide green eyes when he shouted at her, and sat back on her haunches. Once he felt confident that she wouldn't try to follow him, all his attention went to his mission. Andrew disappeared into the charred office area. Feeling his way around, he scorched his hand on a metal file cabinet. He began to cough. It was becoming difficult to breathe, even with the shirt covering his nose and mouth. He was almost blind from the smoke but continued to grope his way toward the desk where the Bible lay. Finally, he put his hand out and could feel its leather cover, still intact. He grasped it and held it close to his chest. The heat was overwhelming and he heard some glass shatter. A piece of ceiling tile fell down right in front of him and he knew that he had to get out quickly. The building was coming down. He turned and headed for the door. Just as he turned, a large wooden beam cracked and splintered and crashed to the floor. Andrew tripped, and landed heavily on the floor. The impact made him gasp, inhaling smoke. He was stunned but tried to raise himself up, to keep going. Horrible pain radiated up from his leg when he tried to stand, and he realized that it was broken, useless. He desperately dragged himself toward where the door should be, but the smoke overwhelmed him. Then he could see two beautiful green eyes watching him. He knew his Taffy was waiting for him. He felt her beckoning him to come to her. With all his remaining strength, he tossed the Bible out the door. As the book landed a few feet from the faithful cat, Andrew breathed his last.

33

TAFFY

Veronica was stunned to see little Taffy outside the burning church, so near to the heat radiating from the structure. Wondering why the cat was there and not at home with Andrew, she called to her. Taffy turned to look at Veronica and then turned back to peer into what used to be the office. The girl ran over to Taffy, and followed the direction of the cat's gaze. She saw an outstretched hand. It was terribly still. Frozen with fear, she stepped back and almost tripped over Taffy. But it wasn't Taffy that she had backed into, it was something she was sitting on, something like a cushion. Veronica didn't have time to worry about that. She had to run to tell the men that someone was in trouble.

"Hey! The girl says there's somebody caught in the building. She saw their hand. Let's go!"

Some of the men put down their buckets. As they rounded the corner, all of them stopped when they saw the little gray and white cat watching the back of the church. The scene was so bizarre, it took a few seconds for them to regain their senses and head toward whatever awaited. Samuel was the first one to recognize Andrew on the floor, motionless.

"Oh God! What was he doing here at this time of night?"

Another man called out, "Look at this!" She's sitting on a big old Bible. And she's acting like it's hers, like she's not going to get off of it."

"What the ....?"

"Why is that out here?"

"How come that cat is on the Bible?"

"That's Taffy, Andrew's cat!"

The men just looked at each other.

"Let's see if we can get Andrew to the store."

It was difficult trying to pick up Andrew to carry him. The heat was overwhelming and the men didn't want to get too close to the burning building. But they finally were able to drag him out and saw that his leg was indeed broken. One man felt for his pulse but there was none. Samuel was so overcome with grief he started to sob. One of the men put his arm around Samuel's shoulders and led him away. The others silently surrounded Andrew's still body. They couldn't leave him there. This part of the building was nothing but embers, but the fire still raged in the front section of the church.

"Come on, we need to get him away from the fire. It will take four of us to lift him," With some difficulty, they lifted him and carried him toward Rosie's store.

After the men left, Veronica walked slowly up to Taffy and reached down to pick up the book, thinking that Taffy would move away from her. Instead, Taffy wrapped her paws around the Bible and wouldn't let go. Veronica reluctantly gave up, but went to tell her grandmother about it. She knew that she should get back to the store anyway; Rosie would be worried about her.

34

QUESTIONS

Chaos ensued. People shouted. The flames burned brighter. The heat intensified. In the distance the sound of a clanging fire truck could be heard. The exhausted local men on the fire line kept up their bucket to bucket transfer of water. The flashing lights drew closer and soon the red truck screeched up to the church. Men piled out, and methodically followed their practiced procedure. No discussion was needed, as each performed his assigned tasks, and they began hosing down the blazing inferno. People had gathered a safe distance away to watch. They saw a group of men carrying what looked like an inert body toward the store. Gasps were heard when a rumor went around that it was Andrew who had died in the fire.

"Oh no!"

"What was he doing there so late?"

"Surely that isn't him!"

A few of the women started crying. One woman fainted. Another started praying, "Oh Lord, please don't let that be our Reverend Maye, and if it is, please let him live."

"First it was his wife and now him."

"Maybe they can revive him."

Four men carried Andrew's body into the store. Rosie was standing on the porch, gripping the railing so tightly that her knuckles were white. She felt as if she couldn't move, as if her feet were made of lead, but she forced herself to walk inside ahead of them and place some empty feed sacks on the counter. Unable to speak, she just gestured for the men to lay Andrew there. Veronica ran in just after the men. Rosie tried to send her upstairs to protect her from the sight of Andrew's body, but Veronica threw her arms around her grandmother and started crying. "I found him, Grandma! I told them!"

Behind the church, one of the firemen clomped toward Taffy and the Bible. He scared the cat and she ran into the part of the woods that hadn't burned. She watched as the man picked up the Bible and stuffed it under his shirt. He carefully examined this section of the building, to confirm that the hose wasn't needed here right away. They would hose everything down one more time before they left. He rejoined his crew at the front of the church. Taffy backed further into the gloom and settled on a log.

Rosie had phoned the local doctor. He was used to emergency calls at all hours, and had grabbed his bag and made the short trip quickly. When he saw Andrew lying still, and the neighbors just standing around, he suspected that there would be nothing for him to do. Rosie had covered Andrew with a blanket, hoping that, somehow, she was wrong, and it still might matter to him.

The doctor took out his stethoscope and listened for a heartbeat. When he had confirmed that there was no heartbeat, he asked what had happened. They explained to him about the fire, and Veronica telling them that she had seen someone on the floor in the church office.

"Doc, is he gone?"

"I'm afraid so. I suspect that he inhaled too much smoke. His leg is broken but that wouldn't have killed him. And he doesn't have any serious burns that I can see."

A couple of the men bowed their heads in prayer.

The doctor asked, "Does anyone know why he was in the church so late? It seems odd that he'd be working in the middle of the night."

"No one knows, Doc."

"There will probably be an investigation, considering the circumstances. We should get him to the county coroner's office. But my guess is that there is no mystery about what killed him, just why he was there at all."

"Andrew had some problems when he was depressed, but lately he was almost back to his old self."

"He was just grieving for his wife then."

Samuel had been quiet during this discussion but now spoke up. "I certainly hope that no one will suspect Andrew of any wrongdoing. He was as good as they come and this community will feel this loss for a very long time."

Some men nodded in agreement.

35

GONE

As Doc predicted, there was a brief investigation. The coroner agreed that smoke inhalation was the cause of death. His presence in the church that night remained a mystery, but there was no indication of deliberate wrongdoing by Andrew or anyone else so his body was released for burial. Meanwhile, the volunteer fireman who had found the Bible turned it in to his own minister, who started making inquiries about it.

They buried Andrew in the church cemetery next to Taffeta a week later. Hialeah had been notified and as soon as she heard the devastating news, rushed to Lighthouse Point to see to his affairs. In all the sadness and confusion, she and everyone else had forgotten about poor little Taffy, who was still hiding in the woods close to the church, but not visible to anyone. She slept underneath a brush pile and tried to fend for herself, catching a few crickets and bugs to eat. She did not venture out to her home where she had lived with Andrew.

She watched the woods as the funeral began, people arriving in their Chevrolets and Fords, all trying to find a place to park along the roadside. She thought about stationing herself at the front door to greet people, as was her habit, but instinctively sensed something was wrong. She knew that Andrew was not around anymore to welcome her to a church service.

Just as when Taffeta had drowned in the storm, it was not only the congregation but people from the whole area who were crowding in for the funeral. The church itself was in no condition for a service, but the weather was pleasant and chairs had been set up in the church yard for the older people who would not be able to stand. It was a somber occasion, with the backdrop of the partially burned building a constant reminder of the pastor's violent death. The smell of charred wood lingered in the air and some people took out handkerchiefs to cover their noses. The building had been roped off with police tape to prevent anyone from entering. Car after car drove up, only to find no place to park. Each one turned around and drove slowly down the road to park behind another mourner farther away. The occupants slowly exited their cars, walked past the ruins, and carefully made their way across the lawn to join their neighbors.

"Dearly beloved, we are gathered here today to pay our respects to Andrew Maye and thank the good Lord for his life of service," intoned a minister from another church, who had volunteered to conduct the service.

Some of the ladies began to weep. A few men wiped their eyes. One of the older men had thoughtfully escorted Hialeah to a chair in the front. Still in shock, she looked blankly around as if she didn't know the purpose of the service. She had spent the past few days going through Andrew's belongings, trying to sort them into piles. Her grief and exhaustion were clearly visible in her haggard visage. Her face was drained of its normal healthy color, and now resembled an expressionless alabaster bust. Her hands were clasped together in her lap and even her black skirt drooped around her calves. Hialeah's normally well-coiffed hair lacked its sheen and hung around her shoulders.

As the minister droned on about glorifying Jesus Christ and Andrew now being received into the company of heaven, Hialeah thought she saw the tip of a gray tail flick in the woods. Her mind returned to the land of the living and it was then she thought of the little cat, Taffy. What had happened to her, Hialeah wondered. She began to feel guilty. She had been preoccupied the past week with other things, and had neglected to check on the cat. She was fond of the cat herself, but, more importantly, she knew that Andrew would want someone to look after Taffy. She made a mental note to look for the cat after the service was over.

Nearing the conclusion, the minister held up a large Bible. "This Bible was found near Andrew's body. We now believe that he went back into the burning church to rescue it, which had belonged to his wife and had been a treasured keepsake in her family."

Hialeah looked up and recognized the book the minister was holding. That Bible belongs to me now, she thought. It had been in the family for years.

"Andrew was so concerned that the old Bible be saved that he risked everything to get it out of the church, thereby losing his life in the process."

Yes, that's right, she thought.

"So dedicated to Taffeta and her memory, he perished in the flames, but found the strength to throw the good book outside so it wouldn't be lost forever."

What's an old Bible compared to one's life, she mused.

"The presiding church board members have decided to pass along the Bible to Andrew's next of kin, Hialeah." The minister walked toward Hialeah and handed it to her. Her hand shook as she reached up to grasp it.

"Always remember the words of our Savior, Jesus Christ, when He said ...."

Hialeah didn't hear the end of the sentence as her hearing had failed her and her mind had gone blank.

She felt faint. She gripped the edge of the chair to steady herself and hugged the heavy book.

The service was over and all the people lined up to murmur their condolences to Hialeah as they passed in front of her. She remained seated and felt the hugs and pats on her back but was numb to their words. She prayed that she could leave and be alone with her thoughts but the line stretched out down the road. Someone brought her a glass of water which she accepted gratefully.

"Thank you. I appreciate you coming. Thank you. I'll be all right. Thanks." She was so tired she thought she'd never see the end of the line. Finally, the last person shook her hand lightly and moved on. The minister walked over to her and sat in the chair next to her. After offering his sympathies, he asked, "Can we pray?" Hialeah nodded silently. He took her hands and said a few appropriate words before he also moved away. She had requested that the casket not be lowered into the ground until all the people had left. When everyone was gone, and she was finally the only one left, the pallbearers lowered the casket into the grave, giving him up to eternity. She was alone now. She had no one else. As she gazed at the hole, slowly being filled with soil, two green eyes watched from behind a tree, not far away.

36

TAFFY'S VIGIL

The people had gone and, after searching briefly for Taffy, Hialeah had returned to Andrew's house. Taffy was alone in the woods. She missed her companion and had been traumatized by the recent events. She had wanted to rescue him from the fire, but the intense heat had driven her back. Some parts of her fur were singed and a couple of whiskers had curled and burned. She tentatively walked over to the newly dug grave and scratched out a shallow place to lie down. Eventually she fell asleep and stayed there for hours, exhausted by her efforts. Some leaves drifted down on top of her and some stuck in the dirt to start decomposing for the winter.

She awakened to the sound of footsteps coming toward her. She darted into the gloomy wooded area and peered around a tree. Taffy watched as Samuel Gass cut a few late-season roses and laid them atop the grave of his friend. He knelt down and put his hand on the area where Taffy had just been sleeping. His head bowed and a few tears dropped onto the ground. He shuddered and pushed himself up and walked away, back to his home. Taffy briefly considered following him home but then decided against it. She wanted to stay with Andrew, whether he was there in person or only in spirit. She had loved him and knew he loved her. He had rescued her in her time of need and she had been able to do the same for him.

37

AFTERMATH

Hialeah was busy sorting through the last of Andrew's possessions. She found that she was able to concentrate better after the funeral than she had been in those first few days after the fire, and now felt that she could complete the task. She knew that his clothes could go to a local charity, and be passed on to less fortunate people. She would use some of his furniture and kitchen items in her cottage. Samuel Gass had promised to help her move whatever she wanted to keep. It would be a comfort to drink tea out of his glasses.

Thinking of tea, she decided to have a glass and take a break from the sorting. She sat at his desk, and idly looked through drawers. Her gaze moved to the book shelves. What on earth would she do with all the books? The religious ones should probably go to the pastor they would hire to replace Andrew. She saw some bound books with no titles on their narrow spines. She was at a loss what to do with most of them. Taking one down, she discovered that it was a journal. A quick look revealed that these volumes covered most of his life. She opened one at random.

> *Dear diary,*
>
> *I have found the love of my life. Her name is Taffeta. We see each other about twice a week and usually walk to a park in Georgetown. Sometime we just walk up and down the hilly streets and admire the architecture of the houses and stores. She does not have a voice, but communicates very well anyway. I think we were made for each other and sometime in the future we may plan to be married. How fortunate I am to have found her.*
>
> *September, 1948*

Hialeah brushed away a tear. She thought about how they really were made for each other and their relatively short married life. If she were still alive today, what would she be doing? Grieving for Andrew, of course, just as she now was. Hialeah flipped back a number of pages to a time in the mid-1930s when Andrew was suffering from the awful headaches.

> *Dear diary,*
> *What is wrong with me? Why do I get*
> *these terrible headaches so often? It's bad*
> *enough that I have to live with Aunt Martha*
> *who doesn't want me. The kids at school think*
> *I'm strange and mostly avoid me. Everything*
> *was so good when my father was here and*
> *now it's turned upside down. What did I do*
> *to deserve this?*

Hialeah wrapped her hands around the cold glass of tea and leaned her head back on the cushion. She thought about how bad Andrew's headaches used to be until he adopted little Taffy.

Taffy! Oh no! How could she have forgotten her again? She knew that Rosie would say, "You've been through so much. It's normal to be forgetful when you are grieving." But she felt guilty all the same. Andrew would want her to take the cat in so she'd have a home. Hialeah pulled on her shoes and quickly walked down the road to the cemetery. It had rained the day before and she found the ground somewhat muddy. As she approached Andrew's grave, she noticed that there were footprints around the gravesite, which probably belonged to people who were paying their respects. A few roses had been laid on top. In amongst the shoe prints, she could barely distinguish a set of what looked to her like small cat footprints. She was no expert, but she was pretty sure. They showed up on top of the grave and from there led toward the woods. Following them, Hialeah lost sight of the tracks in the burned pine needles, ashes and other debris littering the forest floor. She stood there for a moment and considered where Taffy could have gone. The cat was used to living in a house, and having food provided twice a day. Where was she getting her food now? Maybe she was able to catch small rodents and birds. She had lived outdoors with her mother, so perhaps she had taught her to hunt. But even if she was able to catch food, why hadn't she shown herself since the night of the terrible fire?

Hialeah called, "Taffy! Taffy! Come on out for me. Come on, little Taffy."

Taffy didn't come out, but she had hidden herself farther back in the woods and could see Hialeah near the cemetery. Hialeah gave up and went back to the house.

Taffy watched Hialeah leave. Since Andrew had passed away, she had been spending a lot of time on top of his grave. She even slept there, moving under a shrub for protection when it rained. During the daytime, people would come by and stand in front of the gravesite, lost in their thoughts. Some would leave a flower or two. She would hide out in the trees, but close enough to keep watch. A few times she saw Veronica walk slowly around the cemetery, searching. Veronica would call Taffy's name, but the cat preferred to stay near Andrew.

The nights were not to her liking. After living indoors for the years since Andrew had adopted her, she was afraid of bigger night creatures. There weren't many stray dogs, foxes, or coyotes, but she had to always be alert. A bolder cat might have enjoyed the night sounds and the adventure, but not Taffy. Sometimes she would hide underneath the porch of the store. Rosie had seen her a few times, running from the store back to the cemetery. She left some cat food out on the porch and it would be gone in the mornings.

The weather began to shift into winter mode. More days were cold than warm and the sky looked increasingly grey and forbidding. Taffy's coat thickened and her fur grew longer to help protect her against the elements. She was now an outdoor cat, living at the cemetery. She had become skittish and her eyes were wary. She was no longer a friendly and trusting cat. The personality change was evident, but no one was aware of it since she was like a ghost, skittering here and there, disappearing, especially if someone came near. The once-lovable pet cat was turning into a homeless waif. It seemed the only thing she wanted to do was spend time lying on Andrew's grave. She became a fixture there. It was sad to see the cat lingering in the cemetery, sleeping on a grave, to all appearances aware that her beloved owner was now represented by this patch of earth.

Rosie told her granddaughter Veronica to see if her mother would take in Taffy if they could catch her. She didn't want to see the little cat spend the cold winter months outside. Rosie felt a certain responsibility toward the cat, since she had known her since she was a kitten. Veronica still had the kitten's brother, Havoc. Didn't that make Taffy nearly a member of the family? Veronica told Rosie that Havoc may like to have a cat companion, and that his own sister would be a good choice. Rosie agreed that, if Veronica's mother would take in another cat, she would help Veronica catch Taffy.

One day, Veronica sat out in the cemetery, armed with some enticing-smelling cat food. She put it down close to Andrew's grave. She also had brought a box with her to put Taffy in if she was able pick her up. She waited, huddled in her warm winter coat. She read a book while she waited, to give Taffy the impression she was not there to take her away. After about an hour, she detected some movement in the shrubs and out of the corner of her eyes saw a gray and white shadow moving slowly toward her. The cat appeared and stopped, looking at Veronica and then at the food. It had been awhile since Taffy had eaten. Sensing that Veronica meant her no harm, she sidled over to the plate and began to eat. Veronica said in a soothing voice, "Taffy, I want to take you home with me. Will you go with me? I won't hurt you. You remember me from years ago, don't you?"

Taffy kept on eating. Every so often she'd peek over at Veronica. The girl laid her hand on the cat's back and stroked her. Her fur felt rough and wild, not like Havoc's fur, which was soft since she brushed it regularly. But the feline didn't move away.

"Taffy, I want to take care of you. You can see your brother again and be friends."

Eventually, Taffy let Veronica pick her up without a struggle and place her in the box. The lid was closed and Veronica carried her prize to the store. Rosie was delighted that her granddaughter had been able to catch the cat.

"Now maybe she'll be happy again since she'll have a good home. She didn't need to be outside all the time. Let me know how she does, okay?"

Veronica's mother picked up her daughter and the new addition to their family.

38

GOOD FORTUNE

Hialeah was still living in Virginia, working at her job. Since the weather was getting colder and Andrew wasn't around anymore, she spent less time at her cottage in Lighthouse Point. She knew that in the spring she would be back in Southern Maryland, fixing up her little house. Her life revolved around her work, which was demanding of her time. She sometimes thought of little Taffy, about how she was doing and what would happen to her. Hialeah would have liked to have a cat, but she felt she wasn't home enough to be able to give one the proper attention.

One day when she returned home from a particularly stressful day, the phone rang. Picking it up, she heard a woman's voice ask if she was Hialeah Barlow.

"Yes, this is she."

"This is Delores Campbell. I work for Mr. Stringsten, an attorney in Leonardtown, Maryland." Hialeah wondered where this was going.

"Mr. Stringsten wanted me to call you to see if you would be able to meet with him sometime in the next week or so regarding the estate of Andrew Maye."

Hialeah was taken aback, and could only manage to mumble an agreement. They set up an appointment for the following week. She then gathered her thoughts enough to ask what this was concerning, but Miss Campbell said she was not at liberty to discuss it.

"I'll be there next week. Thank you," she said.

The following days were filled with questions, but Hialeah had no answers. What would an attorney want with her, she wondered. Maybe there was some glitch that she needed to take care of. The days dragged on and she requested the day off to drive out to Leonardtown.

When she arrived at the lawyer's office, she was offered a comfortable leather chair and some slightly outdated <u>Life</u> and <u>Look</u> magazines to entertain her while she waited. Fortunately, the wait was short, because she was unable to concentrate on even the simplest magazine article. Her mind kept circling, wondering what this was all about. The secretary smiled and invited Hialeah to follow her into Mr. Stringsten's office. She took note of an expensive-looking Oriental rug and top-of-the-line furnishings. She had been imagining a portly older man, perhaps with a monocle, but the attorney turned out to be less than forty years old, with beautiful white teeth and wavy dark hair. He was wearing a navy blue suit and striped tie. She thought he looked like a movie star. She had no idea of what to say, so she was grateful when he offered her a seat, introduced himself, and immediately opened the conversation.

"You are probably wondering why I asked you to meet with me," he said as he appraised her discretely.

"Well, yes, it's been on my mind ever since Miss Campbell called," she replied.

"I'll get right to the point. I have been your uncle's attorney ever since he and his wife moved to Lighthouse Point, and now I have the sad duty of handling his estate. I want you to know how sorry I was to hear of his passing. Andrew was a fine gentleman and a devoted husband and minister. He was not only my client but he was my friend. We fished together quite a bit whenever I could get away from the office. As you know, he had no other living relatives except for you, even though you were directly related to his wife, Taffeta. Such a tragedy, the way both of them met their demise. Anyway, Andrew left an inheritance to you. He also stipulated that part of the money should be given to Lighthouse Point Methodist Church."

Hialeah sat there dumbfounded. She never dreamed or even thought of what would happen to his assets. This can't be happening, she thought. She had no words to express her astonishment.

"It seems that Andrew's aunt, Martha O'Connor and her estranged husband, who was Catholic, never divorced. Charles O'Connor died without a will, so, even though they hadn't lived together for years, all of his money went to her. By that time she was old and had become stingy with herself as well as with others. She didn't tell Andrew about the money, and spent almost none of it. When she died, he inherited it all. By then he and Taffeta had moved to the parsonage, and were happy with their small-town lifestyle. They decided to hold onto the money for retirement. The only difference that it made in their finances was that they were able to make some anonymous donations to the church."

"You will be receiving a check for the proceeds. The house in which he lived still belongs to the Methodist church so that will be taken care of by the church members.

"I just don't know what to say. I do have a little cottage down the road that belongs to me and I plan to retire there someday, so the money will really come in handy."

"Okay then. We will be in touch with you when the paperwork is completed. Thank you for coming in. If you think of any questions, please call me. I hope to see you again." He smiled kindly at her as she slowly pushed back her chair and turned to exit the office.

"Thanks so much. I guess I'm just in shock, so please excuse me." Hialeah left the office and glanced at Miss Campbell, who was typing at a desk. The secretary smiled and wished her a safe trip home.

The drive back was a blur. Her mind was racing and she had to really concentrate on her driving instead of thinking about the possibilities that were ahead for her. She arrived back at her apartment, just ahead of the Northern Virginia rush hour.

39

TAFFY'S NEW HOME

B ack home in her bedroom Veronica opened the box containing her new acquisition. One green eye appeared above the rim of the box. Taffy carefully surveyed her surroundings, swiveling her head to check out the bed, dresser, and window. She tentatively put a paw on the floor, uncertainly walked over and immediately sprang up to the windowsill. She stationed herself there and gazed out the window.

"Taffy, this is your new home. I hope you'll like it here. There are lots of windows to look out and now you'll be an indoor cat. I'll go get Havoc's brush and see what I can do with your fur." Taffy didn't pay any attention to her.

Veronica left the door open and while she was gone, Havoc sauntered in, still with a faint limp, and stopped, staring at his sister, whom he hadn't seen in years. She turned around and looked back at him and then ignored him to again look out the window. He sniffed the floor and the box and then stood up on his hind legs to sniff Taffy's tail. She swished it away from him. He then batted it with his paw and she hissed at him. It was obvious that she wanted to be outside and wasn't particularly happy being inside this unfamiliar house, especially with this black cat touching her tail. She hissed again just as Veronica came back with the brush.

"Well I see you two have met. Do you remember each other?"

Taffy responded with yet another hiss.

"Oh, come on. This is your brother, Havoc. You can keep each other company while I'm at school. Don't you remember hanging out together at the dock when you were kittens?"

She began to brush Taffy and the cat didn't seem to mind it. Havoc looked on and waited his turn.

Later Veronica fed both her cats in the kitchen. Right after they ate, Taffy went back to the window and perched there, staring into the night. She stayed in this position for a long time, even after Veronica and her mother had gone to bed. When the house was quiet, Taffy went exploring, investigating each room, looking for a way out. She tried to pry open the back door, but it was locked, as were the front door and a side door, leading into the garage. She moved restlessly from one window to another, always looking, always searching.

After a few weeks, Taffy seemed to be adjusting to her new life, but she still spent most of her time on windowsills. She and Havoc were tolerating each other, after the initial shaky introduction. It was a school day and both Veronica and her mother were running late that morning. Veronica left to catch the school bus after her mother had already gone to work. In her haste, she forgot to lock the front door and there was a slight gap where the door met the jamb. Presently Taffy felt a cool breeze wafting in and saw her chance. She pawed the bottom of the door, which opened enough to let her out. Taffy squeezed through and looked around as she gained her bearings. Starting down the long driveway, she trotted purposefully in the direction of Lighthouse Point.

40

MISSING!

Later that afternoon, when Veronica came home from school, as she approached her home's front door, she saw Havoc sunning himself on the stoop. She stopped in her tracks and then saw the front door was open several inches.

"Uh oh," she said to Havoc.

He rolled over on his back, inviting her to pet him.

"Oh no," she said. "Why is the door open?"

He didn't answer; he just blinked his eyes lazily.

Then she remembered Taffy and ran into the house.

"Taffy! Taffy! Where are you?"

Veronica hurried into her bedroom and didn't see Taffy in her usual spot on the windowsill. She quickly looked under the bed and not seeing her cat, checked all the other rooms. Still no Taffy. Outside again, she ran around the house, calling Taffy's name. She looked in the garage and every possible place a cat would hide, to no avail.

Sitting on the front stoop with Havoc, she asked, "What am I going to do now?"

She walked down the driveway, trying to guess where Taffy would have gone. Of course there were no signs of her. She went into the back yard and even searched the field in back of the house. Knowing her mother would be home soon, she wondered what she would tell her. Her mom had been reluctant to take in Taffy but had come to accept her over the past few weeks. Veronica knew she had forgotten to lock the door and her mother wouldn't be happy about that either. Trouble was on the horizon all around.

41

RETURN

Approaching the road, Taffy's senses were heightened. She was aware of the nip in the air, forecasting upcoming cold weather. Her nose caught a whiff of the presence of cows in a distant pasture. She felt the crushed oyster shells on the driveway under her feet and heard a car coming up quickly behind her when she turned into the road. Scurrying into the brush beside the road to avoid the car, she hid until it had passed. Rows of brown and broken corn stalks rose up on the other side of the road, making it impossible to see around them. She continued on her way, paralleling the road, but keeping to its shoulder.

After hours of steady walking, she realized that the sky was beginning to turn dark. Still afraid of the night creatures that might be lurking, she looked for a place to spend the night. Nothing looked suitable until she came upon a dense evergreen shrub, off the road.

Taffy curled up underneath it and kept an eye out for an easy dinner. Wearied from her travels, she instead fell asleep until the morning light awakened her. She stretched and continued on her way, headed toward the river. She wasn't aware of how many miles she covered, and one day was much the same as the other days. Finding food was not easy and she lost a bit of weight. Finding safe places to sleep each night was difficult. Her fur, which had been groomed by Veronica, attracted thorns and burrs, clinging to her underside and back, where she couldn't reach to groom. Some days later, she caught the familiar smell of the river that had been imprinted on her brain since she was a kitten. Her pace quickened and she saw the store up ahead, on her left. She broke into a run, but no one was around to greet her. Continuing through the intersection and spying the cemetery, she scampered straight to her usual place, on top of Andrew's grave. She collapsed and fell asleep, content that she finally made it to her intended destination. Even though it was cold, she spent the entire night in her accustomed place.

Taffy assumed her former routine, as if she had never been taken home by Veronica. Days passed with the cat seeming to guard the gravesite. Nights were spent in the woods, always with a watchful eye cast toward the grave.

Samuel Gass saw her one day when he went to rake up some fallen leaves. He stopped and watched her, surprised that she had come back. He knew Veronica had taken her home and wondered how she had managed to get back to the cemetery. On Sunday, after the church service, two ladies walked into the graveyard to put some flowers on their deceased relatives' headstones. They saw Taffy there and remembered the cat who had belonged to Andrew. It was heartbreaking to see the same cat, almost desperately clinging to the earth, like she was hoping Andrew would come back to life.

"She used to greet us every Sunday as we went into church," one lady said to the other.

"How sad she is. I remember how she would prance down the aisle and take her place up front beside Reverend Maye," the other said.

"I thought someone adopted her. I wonder if anyone is feeding her now."

"I don't know," and they went on their way.

Taffy was content to be back where she belonged. She did show up on the store's front porch, watching for Rosie, hoping for a meal. Later, Rosie spotted the gray and white cat outside and opening the door, exclaimed, "What are you doing back here? How did you get back?"

Taffy's look prompted Rosie to go and find a can of cat food to feed her. Taffy gobbled it as if she hadn't eaten in days, which she hadn't.

"You poor starving little thing! I'll have to call Veronica to see what happened."

That night, Taffy slept on top of Andrew's grave as was her custom. Rosie fed her again. On the weekend, Veronica returned with her box and found Taffy in the cemetery, calmly watching her approach.

"Taffy! Why did you run away? I was so worried about you! It's such a long way to go from my house back here. I thought you liked living with me."

Taffy just slowly blinked her eyes.

"You can't stay out here. It's getting colder every day and you need to be inside. Let me put you in the box so I can take you home, ok?"

Veronica picked up the little cat and gently lowered her into the box. Taffy didn't squirm or try to get away.

And so Taffy spent the winter months living with Veronica, her mother and Havoc. Every day and night she occupied her place on the windowsill, silently watching life go by on the outside.

42

SPRING ARRIVES

The snow was gone and April seemed full of promise, with light green leaves populating the trees and the daffodils following the sun. The winter doldrums had passed and people started to appear in their yards, mowing the wild onions popping up alongside the dandelions in the grass. The newly mown grass smelled pungent but sweet. The first bees foraged for nectar and buzzed the clover. Veronica and her mother were able to let in a bit of fresh air through the window screens.

Veronica's mother stepped outside and smiled up at the sun, appreciating the blue sky and wispy clouds. This was her favorite time of the year, with fall coming in second. Havoc scooted out the door and began to roll around on the concrete walkway, reveling in the warmth.

"What a beautiful day! Do you want your tummy rubbed?"

Havoc peered at her and flopped one way and then the other way. His black coat shone and reflected the sun.

Just then, Veronica came out and immediately reached down to stroke her cat.

"I need to do some shopping in Leonardtown this morning. Do you want to come?"

"Oh yes, I'd like to look at some summer sandals and I really need a new bathing suit too," Veronica answered.

"I suppose you do. You've grown so much since last year, I'll be broke just buying new clothes for you. Ok, we'll leave here after breakfast. Go feed Havoc and Taffy and get dressed."

The mother and daughter spent most of the day shopping and returned home with several bags of clothing and groceries. As they pulled up into the driveway, Veronica saw Havoc waiting for them on the front porch.

She said, "I thought I put Havoc inside before we left. Why is he out here?" A feeling of dread began to creep up into her mind. As soon as the car stopped, she jumped out, unlocked the door and ran inside. "Taffy! Where are you Taffy?" In the bedroom, Taffy wasn't in her usual place on the windowsill, but what Veronica did see was the window screen open at the bottom. Only Taffy would have pushed it out and then escaped.

Veronica felt sick and sat on her bed. She groaned, "Oh no, not again." She knew Taffy was gone, probably making her way back to Lighthouse Point. Her mother was carrying the groceries inside.

"Mom, Taffy's gone. She must have pushed the screen open on the window."

Her mother put the bags on the table and looked at Veronica.

"Do you think she's heading back to Lighthouse Point?"

"Well, probably."

"Let's put the frozen food away and then we'll drive around to see if we can find her."

"Ok. I'm sorry."

"Honey, it's not your fault. I think she just really wants to be back in her place at the cemetery, watching over Andrew's grave. Come on, let's see if we can find her."

As they drove slowly down the road, Veronica asked, "Why does she keep running away? Do you think she doesn't like us?"

"I think that some cats, like some people, just belong in a certain place. Whether they move or are moved to a different place, their heart is still present in their special area. It's a place where they feel most comfortable and at home. Maybe they are missing a person, or their family or their former lifestyle, but the urge to go back is so strong that they do almost anything to return. I'm sure Taffy really likes us, but she feels that she belongs in the cemetery, near Andrew. He rescued her when no one else wanted her and in a sense, she rescued him from his depression. They were bonded, inseparable. If we find her there, we may just need to leave her and maybe your grandmother will feed her and look out for her. I know that may be hard to accept, but we need to consider Taffy's feelings too."

Veronica was silent for a minute.

"But she'll be out in the cold during the winter."

"I'll see if Grandma will fix a bed where she can go in and out of the store. Maybe we can install a cat door somewhere."

Veronica sighed. "Can we drive a little slower so I can keep an eye out for her?"

"Ok, I'll go as slowly as I can, without holding up traffic."

They drove down the road in silence, without finding little Taffy.

43

ON A MISSION

Anyone who noticed the gray and white cat making her way toward her destination would have thought she was on a mission. Determined, she stepped purposefully with her head and tail held high. She knew where she was going and it wasn't back to Veronica's house, as much as she had liked soaking up the comforts of indoor living during the winter months. The changing of the season signaled that she needed a change too. Keeping off the road, as she had the previous year, she picked her way through the undergrowth and weeds. Finding a bit of food was no problem since the warmer weather had beckoned the insects to emerge and enjoy life, unless they became Taffy's dinner.

A spring rain had fallen and Taffy's coat was wet but she didn't seem to mind. The droplets clung to her fur and glistened in the sunlight. She continued on her journey, always heading toward the river.

She stopped to rest and enjoy the warmth, rolling from side to side in a patch of grass. She felt free and her green eyes sparkled with anticipation. She was heading home and back to Andrew! She sprang up and started trotting southward. Taffy felt the river calling her.

Meanwhile, the residents of Lighthouse Point went about their small-town business. Teddy was practicing his basketball skills in his driveway, with a new goal attached to a tree. He wished they had a paved driveway but he had to make do with the crushed oyster shell one. His interest in sports had expanded, and he was learning how to fish from his father's boat.

Bright yellow daffodils adorned the graves of Andrew and Taffeta, as well as some of Samuel's own relatives. The Mr. Lincoln rose bush was leafing out and he was anxious to see the bright red flowers in bloom later in the season. Samuel had removed the winter debris and groomed all the graves before cutting flowers for those who were special to him. He enjoyed having the cemetery looking well-kept, and he hoped that it gave visitors a feeling of peace when they came to pay respects to their loved ones buried there.

Rosie was stocking shelves at the store. She thought about how the store's exterior needed a paint job and wondered whether she could afford to pay Samuel or one of the other men in the neighborhood to do it. She stopped a moment to pour herself a cup of coffee. Sitting down in a chair behind the counter, she started thinking about some of the events that had happened over the past few years. The deaths of the beloved minister, Andrew and his wife, Taffeta had impacted the community in ways no one could have imagined. The accidental burning of the church added to the sorrow, evident in the mood of many residents. It was taking a long time for people to return to the old, carefree way of life in Lighthouse Point prior to the tragedies. The two boys who had unconcernedly thrown their cigarettes on the ground, resulting in so much destruction, had stepped forward and confessed to the act. They had been forced to appear in juvenile court and were required to help rebuild the church. Their parents had also made monetary restitution for the building's repair. The church had yet to hire a new full-time minister so they made do with supply preachers in the meantime.

And yet, some things hadn't changed much. The watermen still made their living fishing. Most mornings, one could hear the sound of outboard motors cranking up for a day's work. The crabs were plentiful and people still caught them off the dock with chicken necks tied to strings. Oysters were still abundant and locals could have as many of the plump delicacies as they could eat, squirted with lemon juice and eaten raw right from the shell.

The forsythias had burst into a bright yellow counterpoint to the bright green spring grass. Yellow and white daffodils nodded lazily toward the sun and other perennial flowers were poking their petals up from the winter's nap. Spring promised new beginnings and Rosie hoped all would be well this year.

The kids still hung around on Friday and Saturday nights, but not in back of the church since the fire. They had moved to the small parking lot in front of the store. This was both a blessing and a curse for Rosie. They spent money buying soft drinks and potato chips but they also left the bottles and empty bags where they dropped them. Rosie had put out a trash can but some refused to take the hint. Every Saturday and Sunday morning, she was out picking up the refuse from the night before.

And Taffy continued on her way.

44

A CHANGE FOR HIALEAH

Hialeah was packing the last of the boxes, getting ready to vacate her apartment in Virginia in anticipation of moving to her cottage in Lighthouse Point. She was embarking on a new adventure and was a bit apprehensive about it. She would be leaving the security of the familiar places she had known for years, like her favorite Italian bakery, right around the corner from her apartment. She would miss the delicious cannoli they made fresh for their customers. She would miss going shopping every Saturday in Alexandria, walking the old streets and dropping into the quaint shops lining the sidewalks. The cobblestone streets still fascinated her and she marveled at their durability. She knew that living in a small town in Southern Maryland would be quite a change in her lifestyle, but then again she was looking forward to the quiet of the river at night, when all the boats had docked at their houses and there was no engine noise to disturb the serenity. Hialeah thought about the laid-back feeling she experienced every time she drove into the crossroads, the way the oyster shell paths beckoned to her and the coziness of her cottage, one of only a half dozen homes on the road. She could picture the rows of geese winging their way across the sky, on their southward migratory journey and the sound of their honking, like a call to line formation. She remembered the wild asparagus that grew along the hedgerow in the spring, making a tasty side dish for dinner, when covered with melted butter or dipped into seasoned mayonnaise. Most of all, she loved the brambles that yielded luscious raspberries in the early summer. She looked forward to picking them every year, in spite of the scratches and mosquito bites. They rarely made it into jam or a pie, because she and her uncle had gobbled them all up with whipped cream, or just by themselves. She smiled sadly to herself, thinking that, now that he was gone, she might share with Rosie instead.

She knew she was making the right decision. Her inheritance would support her for years. Living in Lighthouse Point was inexpensive. She could work part time from her cottage, trying out her dream of becoming a freelance magazine article writer. Uncle Andrew's attorney, Mr. Stringsten, had gone out of his way to be helpful, serving as a sounding board as she sorted out her life goals and calculated what she could afford to do. He was the one who helped her realize that she did not have to remain in her 9-to-5 job in the city. She would forever be grateful that her uncle had left his estate to her. Her thoughts drifted to the cat Taffy, who had been an inherited responsibility. She knew that Veronica had taken Taffy home to live with her and the other kitten. Hialeah would have been glad to keep the little cat herself, but Taffy had not seemed interested in that arrangement. Maybe she would be happier living with her brother Havoc. And no one would have to worry about the cat roaming the cemetery in all kinds of weather.

The movers had already picked up her furniture and belongings so she began carrying out the remaining boxes to her car. The car was packed to the roof with odds and ends. She took one last farewell glance at the place she had called home for so long and backed out of her parking space.

Half a year passed quickly. Hialeah was firmly ensconced in her life at Lighthouse Point. She had made a lot of progress decorating the cottage to suit her own taste. Now, after about six months, she was down to just a few more jobs. Today she was wallpapering. As she finished one wall, she admired the delicate pink roses climbing toward the ceiling, as if entwined in a fence. She thought about Mr. Stringsten, who she now called Karl. In Leonardtown, she had stopped in to see him on her way to the hardware store, and he had taken her out to lunch. She could tell that his interest in her was growing, and she was beginning to think of him as something more than an attorney, or even a friend. Karl had shown some interest in Hialeah, other than that pertaining to her estate business.

She was often at the Leonardtown library to do research for her magazine articles, and he encouraged her to drop in whenever she could. Those excursions were a welcome break from her work on the cottage. All in all, she was very happy with this new life. She was busy, but enjoyed the mixture of tasks that she had developed for herself. The people in Lighthouse Point had welcomed her to town with open arms, because of her relationship to Andrew and Taffeta. Some of the older ladies practically adopted her. She would have been glad for more friends her own age, but she had thought less about that since her friendship with Karl had become more intense.

Several days later, Samuel was on his way to spruce up the church's interior. He glanced over at the cemetery and stopped in his tracks. He couldn't believe his eyes and then shook his head. Sitting atop Andrew's grave, washing her paws was Taffy. It had been many months since he had last seen her and she looked perky and content. She glanced over at him and then continued grooming herself. Walking over to her, Samuel asked, "Well my stars! Look at that! What are you doing back here? I thought you lived with Veronica. Did you run away again?"

Taffy just stared at him and then sauntered over to rub against his legs. He reached down to pet her on the back. Shortly she resumed her accustomed place.

Samuel walked over to the store and found Rosie behind the counter, arranging some cigarette packages displayed on the wall.

"Good morning! Did you know that Taffy was back?"

Rosie turned around and said, "Well I'm not surprised. No matter how many times Veronica takes her home, she's bound to return. She was Andrew's cat when he was alive and she's still his cat even though he's gone. Here, why don't you take her some food? She's probably starving."

Rosie opened a small bag of dry cat food and poured some in a dish and handed it to Samuel.

"Thanks, Rosie."

Samuel took the dish over to the church cemetery and Taffy stood up on her hind legs before starting to chow down on her breakfast.

"What are we going to do with you?" he asked the cat. All he heard was the crunching of cat food. "I know Rosie doesn't want the responsibility of a cat. I'll check with Veronica to see what she wants to do. Oh, hey! Maybe I'll ask Hialeah if she wants to adopt you. She already knows you and she lives all by herself... She might need a cat, just like Andrew did." The wheels were turning in his head. "This is really your place, isn't it? You miss Andrew as much as we all do."

The next day Veronica and her mother pulled up in front of the store. Veronica jumped out and ran over to the cemetery, where Taffy was resting on the grave.

"Taffy, I think you're going to have to stay here. I can't worry about you all the time, trying to get out of the house just so you can come back here. I really thought it would work out, but I can see now that you weren't happy at my house. I love you and want you to be happy. I hate to give you up but I'm here a lot of the time anyway so I'll still see you. This is really hard for me but I want what's best for you. Hialeah said she would take you in and I hope you'll decide you want to live with her. At least you can go to her house to eat and sleep and then you can spend your days here, keeping Reverend Maye company. Will that be ok?"

Taffy gave Veronica a slow blink like she knew what was in store for her.

"Come on Taffy. Let's go down to Hialeah's place now," and she started walking away. Taffy, uncertain, watched Veronica as she headed down the road toward Hialeah's house. She rubbed her face on the grass covering the grave and then sprang up and followed Veronica.

"Good girl! You can come back later once we get you settled in. Oh, you're such a smart cat!" And just as she had done years ago with Andrew, she tagged along behind Veronica to her new home.

Hialeah greeted the girl and the cat even before the knock on the door came.

"Hi Veronica!"

"Hi Miss Hialeah," said Veronica. "I brought Taffy down to you."

Hialeah bent down and picked up the cat, who nuzzled her neck. "Oh, I hope she stays here. I'm so glad to see her again." Hialeah brushed away a tear. "After Andrew died, I saw pieces of his life drift away. Some other people now live in his house, and they've planted different flowers in the front yard. Someone bought his car, and I don't see it around town any more. I was glad that charities could use some of his clothes and furniture, but still it's sad that there isn't any place that I can look at and think of it as his. It's as if there isn't anything solid to show that he had been alive. All I really had left were the memories and some pictures. And of course the family Bible. But now I have a living, breathing beautiful cat to remind me of him." Taffy reached up to play with a strand of Hialeah's hair.

"She just didn't want to stay with us. She wanted to be here, close to Reverend Maye,"

"Well even if she spends time at the cemetery, she can come home to me and know that this is her home just down the road," Hialeah said, as Taffy kneaded her arm. "We'll keep each other company."

Veronica turned to walk away. "Bye, Taffy. I'll be back to visit you."

"Bye, Veronica. I'm so happy to have her with me. Come see us any time."

45

GETTING ACQUAINTED

Taffy stayed the night with Hialeah. She was a bit restless at first, watching the night creatures outside from Hialeah's bedroom window. The new cat owner watched her feline housemate, and knew that Taffy was remembering the free-roaming life she had been living. It wouldn't do to try to keep her inside the house. But she did want to keep the cat inside just for the night, to cuddle with her and to show her that this was home. Around 2:00 a.m. Hialeah woke up to find Taffy curled up beside her in bed. She reached over to pet her and the cat didn't stir. Hialeah fell back to sleep, feeling the most contented that she had since moving into her cottage.

The sun was creeping up over the water and Hialeah could see its rays illuminating the tops of the trees. Taffy was already up and waiting by her food dish.

"Well, I see you know where your next meal is coming from."

Taffy looked up expectantly. She ate her breakfast quickly and then walked over to the door, waiting to be let out.

Hialeah was in a quandary. Should she let her go or try to keep her indoors? She finally decided to let nature take its course and hope for the best. She opened the door and Taffy left her new home and started making her way up the road, heading toward the church and the cemetery.

Hialeah called after her, "Be careful. I'll walk up to check on you later." She felt like she was allowing a preschooler to play with a next door neighbor and she quietly laughed to herself. Since there were hardly any cars on the road, she wasn't worried about that. She was aware that Taffy knew her way around Lighthouse Point, and that it was she who insisted that this town was her permanent home.

At lunchtime, Hialeah took a break and chopped up some leftover chicken. She took the chicken and a small dish to the cemetery and just as she had suspected, Taffy was sitting on Andrew's grave.

"Taffy, I brought you a little snack," as she placed the chicken in front of the cat. Taffy made short work of her snack and began to wash her face.

"Now I want you to come home before dark, ok?" Again, Hialeah thought she was talking to a child but

Taffy seemed to understand her message. Hialeah went home to finish her work and wait for her cat.

As the day wore on, an older lady who was a member of Lighthouse Point Methodist Church stopped by to visit her deceased husband's grave. As she approached the site she saw a little gray and white cat come running toward her. The lady liked cats and stopped to pet Taffy.

"Have you come to say hello? I think I've seen you here before. You're grown now, but you certainly look like the kitten that would follow our poor Reverend Maye to church. Are you the official cemetery watch-cat? I'm just going to visit my Harold's grave for a few minutes. He was a cat lover, you know. We always had one or two around the house and they were good mousers. I miss having a cat but I'm getting on up there in years and a cat would probably outlive me." The lady stopped and thought to herself, "Why am I talking so much to a stray cat? Maybe it's because I'm just lonely without Harold around anymore."

She proceeded to Harold's grave and stood there for a minute reminiscing about all the years they had together. Taffy came up from behind and rubbed the lady's legs. She planted herself on Harold's grave and tucked her paws underneath her.

"Oh that's so cute! Maybe Harold knows you've come to visit him too."

As the lady turned to go, Taffy reached out her paw and was rewarded with a good scratching under her chin.

"I have to leave now but maybe I'll see you here next time."

That evening at dusk, when the spring peepers had started their chorus, Hialeah was preparing dinner and heard a scratching noise at the door. She almost ran to open it for her cat, who was clinging to the screen with all four paws, looking like a pair of old overalls hanging out to dry on a clothesline.

"Oh, you came home! Good cat! Let's get you some dinner too." The sound of the can opener was a signal for Taffy to scent-mark Hialeah with her facial whisker pads.

As the two of them sat down to dinner, Taffy on the floor in front of her dish and Hialeah at her place at the table, the scene was a picture of contentment. They both took comfort in each other's company as Hialeah washed the dishes and Taffy washed her face.

"I'm going to lock the door now so you'll have to spend the night with me."

Taffy meandered through the house, checking out the rooms to see if there were any mice or squirrels hiding in the closets. There weren't any so she hopped up on Hialeah's bed and took a nap. Again, the two spent a cozy night together.

46

THE BIBLE MARKER

Day after day, as the weather warmed, Taffy kept to the same routine. Each morning she would make her way down the road and spend the day on top of Andrew's grave. An old oak helped to shade the area so she wasn't exposed to the hot sun. Hialeah left a plastic dish of water for her so she wouldn't get dehydrated. Taffy's routine was predictable most days, eating breakfast with Hialeah, grave-sitting and returning home at night. Her personality had changed and she became very sociable, greeting people who were visiting the grave sites of their relatives and friends who had passed on. What had been a sad occasion for many now turned into a comforting experience as Taffy brought a little ray of sunshine into their lives. Some of the visitors actually started coming to see her and spent some quiet time with the little cat in the beautifully manicured cemetery. A few would bring some cat treats, which Taffy enjoyed. The church purchased a metal bench and placed it on the perimeter of the graveyard. As the people rested on it, Taffy would jump up to keep them company. She became known as "Taffy, the cemetery cat."

Summer slid into fall and as the days cooled, Taffy's coat thickened and became like a bear rug, but softer. She was a beautiful cat with her gray and white striped markings standing out among the colorful fall leaves. Her green eyes projected a wise and knowing attitude, as if she had seen a lot of life during her years. Growing up nearby on the dock she had witnessed her brother almost lose his life several times, falling into the water, coming very close to drowning under the boat and being hit by a car. She had seen him and her mother adopted, while she had been left alone in a box on the store's porch. Her life had changed when Andrew opened his heart and home to her and she lived contentedly with him until the fire at the church. As traumatic as it had been, watching her beloved human perish in the fire, she had survived and had been taken in by Veronica, who also loved her. But she knew her place was at the cemetery, keeping Andrew company, just as he did with her when he was alive. And now, she had another person in her life, Hialeah, who was delighted to let her live the way she was meant to live.

After an early dusting of snow in October, Samuel was puttering around the grounds, sweeping snowdrifts off the walkways. As he swept his way toward the cemetery, he noticed small cat footprints leading toward Andrew Maye's grave but he wasn't surprised. He did not notice Taffy around however. Instead he saw something colorful on top of the headstone and went over to investigate it. Picking it up, he saw it was some type of cloth that was intricately hand-woven. It measured approximately 10 inches long and 2 inches across. The design was an unusual print of a round orange design on a black background with two crosses at either end. It was such an odd thing to find at all, and seemed even more unlikely against the whiteness of the snow. He held it a long time, wondering what its purpose was and how it could have possibly ended up in the cemetery. The shape reminded him of a bookmark, but he had never seen one that was as intricately woven as this, and he certainly had never seen a bookmark this large. It was clearly a special thing, whatever it was. Someone must have left it as a token of remembrance for Andrew. He returned it to its place on the headstone, and went back to his task of clearing the sidewalks. He hadn't noticed Taffy watching him from behind a tree.

The next day was Sunday. People leaving church after the service pulled on their heavy jackets against the cold spell, and hurried to their cars to head home for a big family dinner. Hialeah, as was her custom, had walked to church but had worn her boots to negotiate any remaining snow. Glancing toward the cemetery, she saw a black and orange object, clearly

visible on top of Andrew's headstone. Carefully nego-
tiating the slick snow patches, she made her way to the
grave. It was the bookmark from Aunt Taffeta's Bible!
She didn't know which seemed more unlikely – that
there was more than one bookmark like this, or that
somehow the one she knew about had gotten from her
house to the cemetery.

She did know that the bookmark had been made
by a long-ago ancestor, and passed down with the old
Bible. Their family wasn't from here, so even if that
relative had made more than one bookmark, there was
no way that it would have ended up in the cemetery.
This must be the one from Taffeta's Bible. Suddenly
she felt a soft bump on her legs and looked down to see
Taffy winding her way around her ankles. She stared
at her cat.

"Did you find the Bible marker and bring it here?"
she asked her.

Of course Taffy didn't reply.

"Let's take it home and put it back where it belongs,
ok?"

Hialeah started walking away and Taffy followed
her. For once she spent the day with Hialeah at home
instead of at the cemetery. Hialeah let the marker dry
on top of a cabinet before replacing it in the Bible.
Her thoughts turned to the significance of the event.
Andrew's cat somehow took the bookmark out of the
Bible that had played such a central role in Andrew's
fatal accident, and then carried it to the cemetery and

placed it on his headstone. That was the only explanation that made any sense at all. The puzzled Hialeah sat in her cozy living room, persuading herself that it must just be some strange coincidence, while Taffy curled up next to her and snoozed away the afternoon.

47

STRANGE HAPPENINGS

Ice started forming along the edges of the river and became permanent, even on those days when a weak sun bravely peeked above the clouds. The East Coast was in winter mode. That included Southern Maryland, in spite of its protected position that let it escape most blustery Nor'Easters.

The residents of Lighthouse Point had made their nests inside their homes, dressing the beds with quilts, storing summer clothes away in attics, and cooking hearty dishes for dinner. The luscious vegetables, so abundant in the warmer months were canned and sat primly on kitchen shelves. Tomatoes, pickles and jellies were lined up, waiting to be opened, consumed and enjoyed until the next season of bounty made the gardeners tired of fried squash, squash casserole, stuffed squash and sautéed squash.

Hialeah was busy pecking away on her typewriter, working on an article for a local publication. The article was about how the old ways of rural Maryland were fading away and how "progress" was turning the area into a more suburban place. She thought about how farms were sold to make way for strip shopping malls and the fields that once grew crops were turned into parking lots. From her experience living in Northern Virginia, she knew the changes were inevitable. That didn't mean that she liked them. And certainly many of the locals bemoaned the influx of new people, who some called "Yankees" even if they hadn't come from up north. Lighthouse Point had been spared so far, but the topic of how nearby areas had been ruined was hotly discussed on the porch of Rosie's store by men bundled up in flannel shirts and heavy winter gear.

After Taffy had helped Hialeah write the article by lying across the keys of the typewriter, she had left to take up her vigil in the cemetery. On colder days, the cat would show up in the afternoons when the temperature had warmed up a bit. Fewer people were coming out to visit her or to place flowers on the graves of their loved ones. But Taffy was still there when they did come, greeting and comforting them and helping to ease their sorrows.

Days passed and it grew colder. Taffy stayed inside on some days and kept Hialeah company. Hialeah had forgotten about the Bible marker until one morning there was a knock on her door. Opening it, she found Samuel on her doorstep.

"Samuel! Why are you out in this cold weather?"

"I just thought you'd want to have this back," he said, holding out the bookmark.

Dumbfounded, Hialeah just stared at it. She then asked him to come in the house.

"You found it at the cemetery again?" she asked.

"Right where it was before."

"It's so strange that Taffy keeps carrying it back there. Why would she do that? It's just plain eerie."

"I just don't know. Maybe she thinks it belongs on the grave."

"Hmmm. She's smart but she's still a cat. I wonder if cats can process that type of information?"

"Well, I'm not an expert on cats but I'd keep an eye on her."

"Thanks for dropping off the marker, Samuel. I appreciate it."

"Stay warm, Hialeah. I'll see you around," he said as he left.

Again Hialeah put the bookmark where it would dry. She was perplexed as to why Taffy would place it on Andrew's headstone, but this time she thought she would outsmart her. Later she replaced it in the Bible and took a small stepladder and put the Bible on the top shelf of her bookcase, where no cat would be able to jump up or climb up to get it. Taffy was asleep in another room and hadn't seen her move the Bible to its place near the ceiling. There was no way the one-foot tall cat could even see the books on the top shelf, much less get to them.

"Let's see if you can find it this time," she said to herself as she looked in on her lazy catnapping feline.

Every week or two, Hialeah would check the Bible, find the marker in it, and congratulate herself on having outsmarted a cat. She found herself wanting to check the cemetery each week as she left church. All throughout the winter she didn't see it, but she would often see Taffy in her self-appointed place. Sometimes Taffy would follow her home but mostly the cat stayed put, keeping her self-appointed vigil, greeting visitors and guarding Andrew's plot. Taffy spent more time there as the weather began to warm up, but still came home every evening to eat and sleep.

Toward the beginning of April, Hialeah was shocked to see that the marker again was decorating the headstone. She wondered how her cat had ever climbed up the bookcase to remove it from the Bible and carry it to the cemetery. And how did she know it was up there? She picked it up and smelled it to see if it had a distinct odor but she couldn't detect any. Of course cats have a more refined sense of smell than humans do, but she still couldn't believe that this was happening. So once again she took it home with her. Taffy was still at her post and Hialeah was home alone. She carried the stepladder to the bookcase and removed the old Bible on the top shelf. After searching through the good book for a few minutes, she found the passage she was looking for and placed the marker in the book of Proverbs, chapter 12:10. "A righteous man cares for the needs of his animal..." She thought that was an appropriate verse for the situation. Climbing back down the ladder, she was thinking of where she could hide the Bible this time. In her bedroom was an antique chest of drawers that had belonged to her grandmother many years ago. It was a beautiful piece of furniture made of burled oak and was highly polished. A beveled mirror was attached to the top and three drawers held her sweaters and various items of clothing. The bottom drawer could be locked with a small key. She never had the need to lock it but now she took the key which was hidden on the bottom and placed the Bible with the marker in the drawer. She then put some clothes that she rarely wore on top of it and shut the drawer and locked it. She made sure to test it to see that it really was locked. Taking the key to her desk, she hid it in a drawer that held scissors, tape and pens. Feeling somewhat smug and somewhat silly, she went to the kitchen and made a cup of tea.

Several weeks passed and again, Hialeah forgot about the Bible and its bookmark. She was reveling in the new warmth of the spring season, after an especially long winter. She decided to plant some flower seeds in her small garden and found her rake and trowel in the back utility room. Raking the winter debris gave her a feeling of accomplishment as she hauled the twigs and fallen leaves to her side yard. She uncovered a stand of wild asparagus, poking their bullet heads up close to her fence. She snapped off a dozen stalks, carried them into the house and placed them in a glass of cool water in the refrigerator, to be cooked later that day.

This morning Taffy had stayed around the house instead of going to the cemetery and she followed Hialeah around the yard, rolling in the dirt and acting like a playful kitten, Finally, she raced around in circles before running up a small maple tree. She perched on one of the lower branches and stared down at Hialeah who laughed at her.

"Come on down here, you silly cat," she said. Taffy blinked at her and pawed at the rough tree bark. "I don't know if you've ever climbed a tree. Now how are you going to get down?"

Taffy wasn't in a big hurry to return to earth. She was having fun watching birds fly by and listening to their songs. Hialeah scattered her marigold seeds in the flower bed and covered them with a bit of soil.

"I'm going to get the watering can, so you stay put for a minute, ok?"

When she returned to water her seeds, she noticed that Taffy was no longer in the tree. Obviously, the wild cat had figured out how to climb down somehow. Since the day was so pleasant, Hialeah decided to take a walk to get some exercise and went inside to change her shoes. First she meandered down to the river, taking the shortcut through some bushes. The water was calm and Hialeah sat down on the ground for a minute to adjust her shoelaces and focus on the peacefulness of her surroundings. She thought about her former life in Northern Virginia and how different everything was here in this small Southern Maryland town. Now that Karl was in her life, Hialeah knew that her life was fairly complete. She had no regrets about moving. If she wanted some excitement, she would drive back to Alexandria to visit some friends for a day or two. She could shop and buy things that weren't available in Lighthouse Point and get her fix of the never-ending traffic and nightlife and then return home to her beloved cat and home.

Leaving the path for the road, Hialeah headed toward the store. She found Rosie in her usual place behind the counter, visiting with one of the regular customers. Both women greeted Hialeah as she came in. "How're things going with you?"

"Very well, thank you."

"Have you been over to the cemetery today?" Rosie asked.

"No, not yet. What's going on?"

"That Bible bookmark is back on Andrew's head-stone, that's what."

Hialeah stopped and her face turned white. She couldn't believe what she just heard.

"No, that can't be," she cried. "I hid it and locked it up so Taffy couldn't find it!"

"Well, maybe you need to see it for yourself. I'm pretty sure it's the same one that kept appearing there last year," Rosie said.

"This is unbelievable! How can this happen? There's no way that she could have found the key and unlocked the drawer and taken the marker out of the Bible."

"I don't know, honey. Maybe someone else is doing this."

"But who? No one has been in my house besides me and no one would have known where I hid the key." Hialeah was getting more agitated and uneasy.

"Come on over here and let me get you a cold drink."

Hialeah's head was spinning and she felt out of control. Was she going crazy? Did she just imagine that she had hidden the marker some time ago? Should she be scared? What the heck was going on here?

Rosie said, "Let me walk over to the cemetery with you. I suppose it will still be in the same place." Hialeah was grateful for her help and understanding.

As they neared the plots, Hialeah could see her cat Taffy relaxing on top of Andrew's grave. Grass had covered it, as well as Taffeta's grave next to it.

"Taffy! Are you the one who keeps putting the marker on the grave?" she cried. Taffy just gave her a long look and rested her head on her paws. "This is crazy! I just can't believe this."

Sure enough, the same bookmark was draped over the top of the headstone. Hialeah picked it up and examined it, noticing the intricate beaded work on the material someone had done long ago. There were two crosses on either end and some pattern in the middle that looked like a circle or a path that led to one of the crosses.

She handed it to Rosie who looked at it intently. "I believe that this circle is a labyrinth. People walk around it to the center as a meditative tool. It's an ancient way of praying and sometimes people make them out of rocks. Look, it seems that one end either leads to or from the cross."

Hialeah again studied it. She had thought of it as an abstract design, but hadn't realized it might be a picture depicting a path, but now she saw what Rosie was talking about. She looked at Taffy and back to the marker. It still didn't make any sense.

"Maybe you should just leave it here instead of taking it home with you. Maybe Taffy thinks it belongs here."

"Rosie, this is just too much for me to understand. I guess I'll leave it here. I'm going to check my drawer at home just to make sure that it's really not there. Come on Taffy, let's go home. Thanks for everything, Rosie."

The woman and the cat padded down the road. Hialeah was deep in thought, wondering whether she was witnessing a miracle or something else. When she got home, she went to her desk for the key. It was exactly where she had left it. She unlocked the dresser drawer. The Bible was underneath her clothes, which did not seem to have been disturbed. But the bookmark was missing. She made herself a cup of tea and sat down at her kitchen table, staring at Taffy. Taffy stared back. When Hialeah picked her up, Taffy wrapped her arms around Hialeah's neck, nuzzling her and rubbing her fuzzy face into her hair.

48

AN EXCEPTIONAL CAT

The Bible marker remained in place for years. It finally started to disintegrate from exposure to the weather, its brilliant colors fading and the material unraveling. Taffy kept up her vigil, consoling mourners who visited the cemetery. What an unusual little cat she was, soothing their pain, greeting them and being a comfort to all who had lost their loved ones. Her green eyes expressed an understanding that made her look like she was very wise. The residents of Lighthouse Point looked forward to seeing her and sometimes took some catnip or a special treat to her. She brought much joy to Hialeah, who treated her like she was her furry child. She knew this was a special cat with special powers and she was privileged to share her life with her. After a while she stopped wondering why the marker kept appearing on the headstone. She just accepted the fact on faith that it belonged there, along with the little gray and white cat. She decided that, although she had no rational explanation for what was happening, it was a blessing. She had no choice but to let it remain a mystery, but she no longer worried about it.

49

A RETURN TO LIGHTHOUSE POINT

Approximately twenty-five years later on a crisp fall Saturday morning a shiny late model sports car pulled up at Lighthouse Point Methodist Church and parked in the paved parking lot. The car bore license plates from Virginia. The driver emerged, a middle aged lady, who stood there beside the car gazing at the church. She had short blonde hair and was stylishly dressed in jeans and an expensive looking jacket.

The door opened on the passenger side and a pretty teenager hopped out. The girl strongly resembled the woman, except that her long blonde hair was pulled into a ponytail. Her green eyes took in the peaceful scene. She walked around the car to stand by her mother.

"This is where your great uncle preached. Maybe we can go inside." Walking toward the front door, Hialeah noted the changes that had taken place over the years. The grounds were well-kept but the rose garden was gone. The building itself looked maintained, and a new wing had been added on the side. Instead of wooden siding, the outside walls had been bricked, which made the building look indestructible. Hialeah wondered whether bricks would have prevented the fire from burning the old church, or at least kept it from killing her uncle. But the past couldn't be rewritten. She turned her attention to the door handle and was surprised to find it locked.

"Oh too bad. I wanted you to see the piano that Taffeta played."

"Let's look around outside instead," said the girl.

"I don't know," Hialeah hesitated. "How about if we walk around the neighborhood for a bit? I'm not sure I can handle it yet."

"Ok."

They walked over to where the store used to be. The building was still there, but had fallen into disrepair. Paint was peeling from the its side, and one window had been boarded up. The hand-lettered sign on the front door said "**Closed. For Sale.**" A Maryland phone number followed. The steps up to the front porch were rotting. Watching where they put their feet, they crossed the small porch and peered in through the front window. After their eyes adjusted to the dimness of the interior, they saw the same shelves with a few cans of food lining them, like old soldiers awaiting their orders. The wooden floor had darkened and was worn down from the many feet that had trod it over the years. The store looked smaller, somehow, than it did during its heyday. The cash register was still there but the ice cream cooler was gone. Gone too was the slot machine.

"Sweetie, this place was the hub of the neighborhood. It's where people gathered to see their friends, and where they came together when sad things happened." She remembered something and turned around to see that the old bell was still attached to the post outside. It had rusted over the years, but looked like it could toll a pretty good Bong! Bong!

"When there was an emergency, someone rang the bell and it called the men together. When your great aunt Taffy drowned after the big storm, the watermen searched for her but couldn't find her."

"Tell me again how she drowned," the girl said.

Hialeah recounted the story and Taffeta Marie listened attentively.

"That's pretty sad. I guess Andrew was upset for a long time."

"For a very long time."

They walked down the old steps and turned into what used to be the shell pathway. It was now a one-lane macadam road. At the end, where the rickety dock had been, there was nothing but a small metal marker, and the river gently lapping at the shore. Taffeta Marie read the words out loud:

> *On July 30, 1960, Tropical Storm Brenda made landfall on the Potomac River. Strong currents and near hurricane-force winds swept through the southern part of Maryland producing a small tornado which destroyed many residences in Lighthouse Point. One person died as a result of the unusual weather event.*

Hialeah stood motionless as her daughter spoke the somber words. Silently they moved closer together and Hialeah put her arm around the girl.

The pair continued along the road, which curved to reveal several large new houses. They were situated to provide views of the water, and sturdy docks jutted out from their back yards. One had a Bass Tracker tied up to it.

The green fishing boat with Taffy's name on the side was gone, of course. There was no point in mentioning it to Taffeta Marie. They retraced their steps, taking the road past the church to the house where Andrew and Taffeta had lived. It was impossible to see what the house looked like now, because there were large shrubs concealing the yard. There were big stone columns on each side of the driveway, and a gate across it, suggesting that strangers were not welcome. Hialeah sighed softly.

The changes she had seen so far made Hialeah nervous about what she might find at the site of her cottage. Had it been torn down? Or just left to go to pot? She walked more slowly, hanging back a little. Taffeta Marie spotted the building first, and exclaimed, "Oh! How cute!" Hialeah was relieved to see that not only had the cottage not been torn down, but it was being well cared for. The little front yard was planted with flowers that were blooming since there hadn't been a killing frost yet. The asters and black eyed Susans made a pleasant contrast. A white picket fence enclosed most of the area. A red pickup truck was parked in the side yard, with a child's bicycle beside it.

"This is it!"

"Your cottage, Mama?"

"It sure is. I spent many a day working on it to get it in shape. I have a lot of good memories of this house."

Hialeah took the camera from the strap around her neck and snapped some pictures of her former home.

"I'm glad to see it's still standing and they haven't changed it very much."

There were more houses than there had been when Hialeah left, but a sense of quiet pervaded. The owners were probably summer people from DC who spent weekends at their river retreats. Hialeah was glad that it seemed the people in her house were year-round residents.

"Let's go back. I think I'm ready to show you the cemetery."

They walked slowly back toward the church, with Hialeah pointing out new river front homes that weren't there in the 1960s. She remembered walking this same road on Sundays, with little Taffy following her to church. She hesitated, and Taffeta Marie looked up at her and said, "What's wrong, Mama?"

"Oh, this is sort of emotional for me, walking down memory lane. I'll be okay in a minute."

Coming up on the back side of the church Hialeah pointed out the place where the old family Bible had been found after the fire. She said, "It is still amazing to me that the Bible was in such good shape after Andrew threw it outside while he was suffocating from the smoke inside the office."

"I know why that Bible was important to him, but I still don't understand why anyone would die to save a book."

"You have to remember that he had no intention of dying. He thought he would come out with the Bible. If the building hadn't started collapsing just then, he would have gotten out just fine. I think he decided that the Bible was important enough to go into a scary place, with flames around him, and risk getting burned."

"He was very brave, wasn't he?

"Yes, he was, sweetie."

Trying to lighten the mood a little, for her own sake as well as Taffeta Marie's, Hialeah continued, "And you know he's the reason that I met your dad. They were longtime friends, and he helped me so much after Uncle Andrew died."

They approached the church's cemetery. Hialeah could see that the basketball court was gone, replaced with more paved parking area. The woods that had formerly been behind the church were now someone's grassy yard. More headstones had been added to the lot over the years. As they wandered the cemetery, they came to two relatively recent headstones side by side. Both were engraved with GASS in large letters. One had Samuel's name and the other had Claudia's. Hialeah paused and said a quick silent prayer, remembering, with great gratitude, Samuel's friendship with her uncle.

A bit further down they came upon Stan Teeter's grave. His teeth weren't there. Hialeah recounted the stories of his false teeth to her daughter and they both laughed.

Toward the front of the cemetery they saw three headstones lined up in a row: TAFFETA MAYE and the one next to it read ANDREW MAYE. A smaller one next to Andrew had a cat engraved on it with the inscription, *Taffy - Beloved and faithful companion, forever in our hearts*

Both stood there for a long time, lost in their thoughts. Hialeah put her hand on the little cat's grave and a tear rolled down her cheek. So many memories....

"Someday I'll tell you the story about the Bible marker."

"Ok. I love to hear stories about the olden days."

Finally, the girl asked, "Are you ready to go Mama?"

"Yeah I think so, Taffeta Marie. Your dad will be wondering about us."

As they drove slowly away, a lone blue crab tugged at the chicken neck in the metal trap. The trap was fastened to the piling at the end of a fancy new dock, jutting out from a well-manicured back yard. Unaware of its plight, the crab concentrated on removing the bits of chicken still attached to the tender bones of what remained of last night's dinner. The crab was large enough that it would not have to be released to continue its life without threat of becoming someone's feast. The trap moved with the motion of the water, creating a small stir that was visible on top of the water. Unbeknownst to the crab, a pair of emerald green eyes were watching its every movement. A gray and white paw reached down to touch the water. The cat quickly withdrew its arm, and began methodically licking her paw to remove all the offending moisture. The feline stretched out at the end of the dock, taking in the sun's rays. What a picture of contentment she made, languorously enjoying her life, slowly blinking her eyes as she looked skyward.

A cat comes into your life to nourish your soul and heal your heart

EPILOGUE

What happened to the green eyed kitten, and to the humans and cats who shared her life, during those twenty-five years between her adoption by Hialeah and Hialeah's visit to Lighthouse Point with her daughter, Taffeta Marie?

Veronica's black cat Havoc never entirely gave up his mischievous kitten ways. In spite of having used up most of his nine lives in his first few months of life, he lived to be more than eighteen years old. He chased butterflies around the yard, batted Veronica's mother's knitting around the room, and knocked things off the mantle. But he never ventured out of their large yard into the street.

Veronica followed through on her dream of becoming a veterinarian. She had made good grades at the

University of Maryland, and became the first woman to enroll in the University of Georgia veterinary school under the special arrangement between the two states. After graduation she set up a practice in Washington, D.C., specializing in the treatment of cats.

Teddy, Veronica's childhood friend, stayed in Lighthouse Point after graduating from high school, and became a commercial fisherman. He became known as the guy who would take in stray cats, and even the occasional dog. He went dancing every Friday night in Leonardtown. Every now and then he and Veronica would have their own little reunion. They would drive up to Marshall Hall and ride the merry-go-round in the amusement park, or wander around eating cotton candy and reminiscing.

Samuel Gass continued to maintain the church grounds as long as he was able. He could be seen every Sunday in his favorite pew, listening intently to the sermon or taking a short catnap. He and Claudia celebrated their 60th anniversary in the fellowship hall of the new church. Not long after, she died peacefully in her sleep. Samuel followed her after only a few weeks.

Rosie continued to manage the old store for years. She observed the changing town, older residents passing away while few new year-round people moved in. The townspeople who did stay generally worked in some nearby town, and drove there to buy their groceries. She was barely selling enough in the store to cover expenses, and she was feeling her age. It seemed as if nearly everyone she had known had died or moved away. One day she put a "For Sale" sign in the window. One of the teenagers, now grown, who used to hang out on the benches out front bought it, planning to turn it into a video arcade for the next generation of kids. As soon as the sale was complete, Rosie moved to a condo in Ocean City.

Hialeah loved her cottage and loved her years living in Lighthouse Point. She gardened and wrote her freelance articles. She and Karl Stringsten became seriously involved. He came for dinner or took her out to a Leonardtown restaurant at least once a week. Karl would sometimes hint at them marrying and her selling the cottage, but she was not interested in that idea as long as she was the steward of Taffy. The little cat was a blessing to everyone who visited the cemetery. Hialeah felt grateful to be able to share her life with such a sweet and gentle creature, and wanted to enable Taffy to stay there, where she could guard Andrew's grave. Hialeah felt that the cat was a living link to her aunt and uncle, and she would stay as long as Taffy needed her. The morning when she discovered that Taffy, peacefully curled in a ball on the bed beside her, was not breathing, she called Karl. She was so heartbroken that she couldn't explain what was wrong, but when he heard her crying, he hung up the phone and drove straight to her cottage. The seriousness with which he took her loss, when some other man might have laughed at her for being so attached to a cat, cemented her attachment to him. Not long after they married, she sold her cottage, and they moved to Georgetown, where he set up his new law firm. They attended the church where Andrew had met the mentor who encouraged his interest in the ministry. After a few years they had a baby girl, and named her Taffeta Marie, after Hialeah's beloved aunt.

Taffy enjoyed the perfect life for her temperament, being pampered by Hialeah while also being allowed to follow her own impulses. She continued to keep Andrew company with her visits to the cemetery and she greeted all visitors there. But she never again attempted to enter the church on Sunday morning. She didn't station herself at the door of the new building to welcome the congregation. A few times a week she would wander to the store to silently greet Rosie, who kept a bag of dry cat food handy for her. Less often, if someone was crabbing or fishing off the dock, she would sit beside them and look at them until they offered her a cricket. She was a very contented cat.

Lighthouse Point continued to be a rural retreat and drew more people from the Washington area on the weekends as a getaway. People trailered boats and put in at a new access up the road. They would putter around on the water, fishing, sailing or just enjoying the tranquility of the river. A few people water skied, leaving their docks and flaunting their skills. Life went on as before but there was never another weather incident as severe as the one that happened in 1960. Older houses were sold and many were demolished to make way for larger ones, especially those built at the water's edge. Some preservation-minded people banded together and created a small museum, dedicated to the watermen who had made their living fishing, crabbing and oystering years ago. Some residents donated old fishing gear, crab traps and photos to tell the story. In one corner, locked in a wooden case, was a small piece of faded green wood, with the letters T A F F Y that were barely visible painted on it. They collected enough funds to have the small metal marker installed near where the old dock had stood, detailing what had happened during Tropical Storm Brenda. Visitors to the Lighthouse Point Museum found the place charming and after examining the artifacts, sometimes strolled around the small neighborhood, imagining what life had been like so many years ago. They weren't able to envision the heartache and misery that the storm and later, the fire that destroyed the church, had wrought upon the community, however. Taffy the cat's story had been memorialized in a newspaper article that was displayed in the museum. A few people walked over to the aging cemetery to check on the graves of Andrew and

Taffeta. Most loved to see little Taffy's headstone, positioned right beside Andrew's. She had been buried beside her beloved human, now both together in the next life, where people and their pets were reunited for all time.

   **Proverbs 12:10 A righteous man cares for the
            needs of his animal..."

Made in the USA
Columbia, SC
02 October 2017